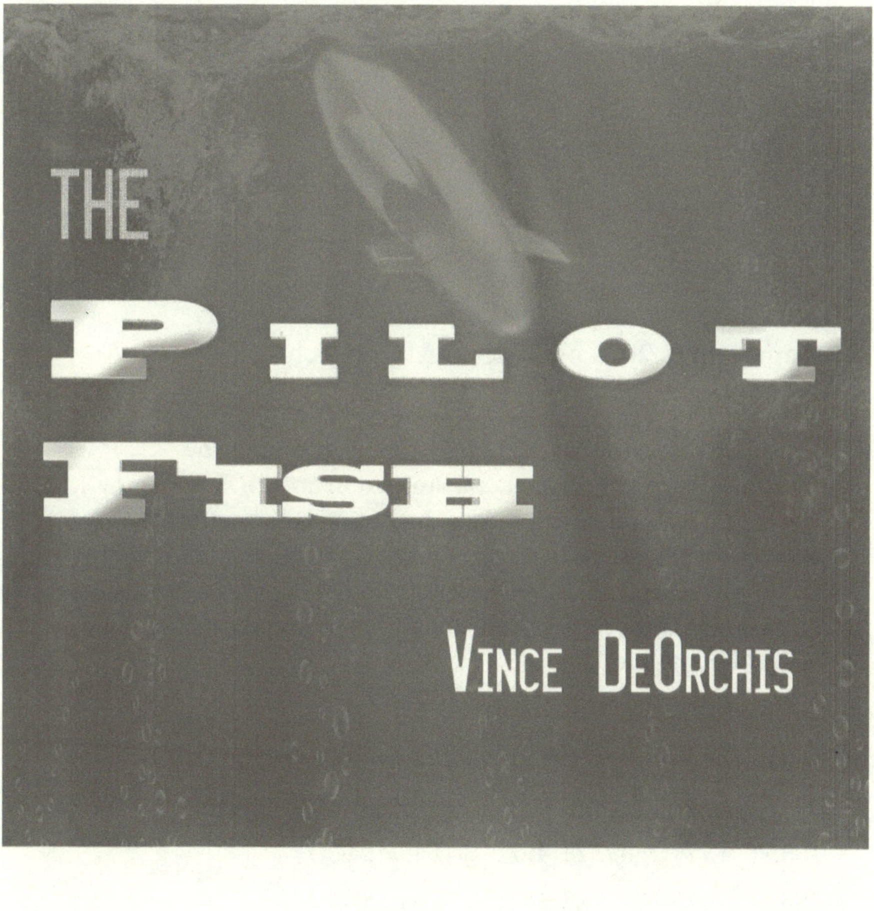
THE
PILOT
FISH
VINCE DEORCHIS

Library of Congress Control Number: 2025914863

ISBN: 979-8-89228-497-4 (Paperback)
ISBN: 979-8-89228-681-7 (Hardcover)
ISBN: 979-8-89228-496-7 (eBook)

Printed in the United States of America

DEDICATION

This novel is dedicated to all the great maritime lawyers I have worked with, and against, during my forty-plus years of law practice. It is a wonderful and imppressive bar, and as one federal judge has remarked, "filled with gentlemen."

ACKNOWLEDGMENT

I would like to acknowledge and thank the invaluable help of Fred Kuffler, Wook Chung, Bob Furjanic, A. Dalia DeOrchis Pucci and my brother, Dr. Douglas DeOrchis, all of whom gave me their precious advice and time in their review of this novel.

Prologue

Thwack! The meaty, open palm of the right hand smacked against the jawbone, crushing the irritating mosquito into a pulverized bloody pulp that was now embedded in parts of the unshaven cheeks of Captain Kris Marzak, a forty-five-year-old Master of vessels.

The captain smiled with satisfaction at the execution of the bug that had been annoying him for more than a half-hour. It was rare to have a flying insect on the bridge of a 40,000- ton bulker vessel, but it was the dead of summer, and the English Channel was humid with a thick blanket of fog and absolutely no wind. Perhaps the tens of thousands of tons of unbagged fertilizer in the ship's holds had attracted the mosquito this far out to sea.

Well, thought the captain, *now it won't have to fly back to land.* He picked up a half-empty cup of coffee from the pilot table and used a stained paper napkin underneath to wipe the reddish smear off of his cheek.

Captain Marzak, licensed to sail vessels of all sizes and tonnage on all seas, never let his eyes wander from the large glass windows overlooking the ship's forward deck. A white light mounted on a pole at the tip of the bow glowed like a five-pointed Christmas ornament in the haze and thick air, pointing the way in a sea that was deadly quiet and dark grey. It was nearly two in the morning, yet the Master had been on the bridge since sunset, keeping alert for other vessels hidden in the milky fog that engulfed the English Channel. Meanwhile, his second officer was carefully studying two radar screens mounted in the middle of the bridge room, each set for a different distance. The young officer marked the targets on the screens with a keyboard so that the ship's computers could track the paths of other vessels nearby. White lines drawn by the computer streaked across the radar screens, showing the bearing and distance to moving objects that were more or less keeping to their side of the road in the busy channel. Nearly a dozen ships were cautiously moving under reduced speed and with extra lookouts.

"How is she handling?" asked the captain as he took a swig of the now cold and tasteless coffee.

The helmsman, a skinny twenty-eight-year-old Philippine seaman with dark stringy hair, momentarily took his eyes off the compass ball mounted on the ceiling and turned to face the captain. "She is handling well, Captain. We are on course, with little current and no wind. Do you want me to put the ship back on auto-pilot?"

"No, no. God only knows what could come out of this fog. I am especially worried about the fishing boats. We won't see them on the radar until the last minute. Keep steering. Hopefully, this fog will lighten up by morning."

The ship, named the *Viking Trader*, continued to glide noiselessly through the still water at about nine knots. The deck lights had been turned on all around the ship but the bright lights were quickly absorbed and distorted by the sticky fog. Occasionally, the crew blew her fog horn, and like a mating call, other ships could then be heard responding in the distance, each giving fair warning. The heavy air muffled the deep bass sounds, skewering any effort to accurately detect the direction from where the horn blasts originated.

"Captain, we should be arriving off the port of Le Havre before noontime at this speed. Weather forecast doesn't help. More fog and some showers at daybreak," remarked Second Mate Erik Nils, who continued to stare at the radar screens. After a moment of silence, he added, "The screens are good. Everyone is keeping their distance. But we do have a ship off our port stern, several miles behind us. It must be moving at nearly eighteen knots. Looks like she will be passing us within a half-hour."

"Idiot," said Marzak. "Moving at high speed in this fog is just foolish. Keep an eye on her."

The *Viking Trader* continued to slip cautiously through the water with little wake. It had been over two weeks since Marzak and his crew had left Venezuela where the fertilizer had been loaded. Their ship had encountered several days of heavy weather in the Atlantic, which delayed their crossing. The captain was calculating how many more days it would be before he could start his four-month shore leave. He grinned. Twenty days, that was all that was left. He looked in his cup and realized it was time for some fresh brew. "Going to run down to my cabin for some good coffee. I'm tired of the crap that's brewed up here. I'll be right back." With that, the lean and weathered officer briskly walked through the door in the back of the wheelhouse and took the stairs down one level to his cabin.

Erik continued making calculations on the chart and plotting the next course change. A few minutes later, a warning light went off on the radar screen. He looked closely at the monitor. The warning indicated a potential collision course. The target, which was the vessel following behind them, had changed from a white marker to a red marker. It was still well off to the left side of the *Viking Trader*, but the target was slowly drifting in their direction as it raced forward in the blind sea. The Mate noted that the advancing vessel's automated identification signal was missing, which was against international safety laws. Erik clicked on several keys and waited for the program to re-calculate the collision course. New lines, drawn in red, appeared on the screen, indicating that the courses of the two vessels would intercept in about twenty minutes. At that moment, Captain Marzak walked back onto the bridge, enjoying the steam and wonderful aroma rising from his full cup of French roasted beans.

"Captain, got a problem. Radar indicates that the ship behind us, which is off the AIS system, is drifting into our lane. We will be on an intercept course in about twenty minutes."

"OK. Let's reduce speed by two knots and let her get in front. God knows where she is in a rush to go to in this weather, but let's get out of her way."

"Aye, Sir. According to the computer, the reduction in speed should do it. Shall we stay on our course of 270?" the Mate asked.

"Yes. Stay on course. Not a lot of room in this part of the Channel. We don't need to end up on the rocks." The captain rang up the engine room and gave the order to reduce speed. He then made an entry in the logbook about his order. Marzak glanced over the charting table and saw that there were some pages sitting in the fax machine. He pulled out the paper, which was mostly the latest weather maps. However, there was also a communication from the head office in Oslo about the next charter, which would start after unloading the fertilizer at Le Havre. Marzak smiled when he saw the trip was from Greece to Bremerhaven with a load of iron ore. That would put him in an excellent position to fly home for his vacation leave.

The high-pitched emergency alarm on the radar suddenly went off again. The nervous junior officer looked at the radar and turned to the captain. "That ship is getting closer, still swinging towards us, and she is not slowing down. Our speed change won't work. It is still on a collision path."

The captain calmly walked around to the radar and looked at the large screens. The vessel behind them was now less than a mile. What was interesting was that the path recorded by the radar showed the ship was not sailing a straight line, parallel to the other ships in their lane, but instead was on an arc that seemed aimed at the *Viking Trader*.

Marzak picked up the handle to the VHS radio phone. He turned to Channel 16 and holding the send button, clearly and firmly stated, "This is the bulk ship *Viking Trader* on course 270, speed seven knots, headed towards Le Havre. Will the vessel on course 305, less than a quarter of a mile behind us, please identify itself and change course. This is an emergency. You are on a collision course with our vessel." He let go of the send button and adjusted the gain dial to make sure the radio was working while he waited for a response. Static was the only thing that could be heard. He repeated the message, and again there was only silence on the marine radio.

"Eric, get on the ship's horn and sound an emergency blast," the captain ordered before walking briskly towards the wing extension of the bridge that hung out over the port side of the ship like a giant balcony. He stepped through the door and immediately felt the heavy and damp air surround him. There was little sensation of the ship moving and the heavier patches of fog just swirled around the edge of the ship's hull and over the deck. The deep rumble of the ship's horn sounded, seven times, and was immediately lost in the dense white cloud that hung over the water. Marzak looked aft and searched carefully for any signs of the approaching ship. He left the binoculars hanging from his neck. They were useless as visibility was less than one hundred feet. He headed back into the bridge house.

"She's still coming right at us," said the mate, with growing nervousness in his voice. His face was glued inches from the radar screen in hopes that he would soon see electronic proof that the other ship was correcting its course.

"Helmsman, take her to starboard. Course 285. Eric, tell the engine room to come to a full stop. It's too late to outrun that ship. Hopefully, she will overshoot our course."

The captain pressed the emergency horn button himself, sounding the alarm again.

"Captain, she is less than a hundred yards away, and still turning towards us!"

"Christ, almighty. Alert the crew and tell them to grab life jackets." The captain gave up on the horn and ran to the VHF radio and picked up the handset. "Unidentified ship, you are on an imminent collision course with us. Change course to port. Please resp…." Before the captain could finish the sentence the fog parted outside the windows on the left side of the ship. The towering dark bow of a container ship came into sharp focus as it barreled its way towards the *Viking Trader.*

"Helmsman, hard over to starboard, hard over... Hold on…"

Although the *Viking Trader* was still making some speed with her engines cut, the time to turn was painfully slow. Marzak was surprised that the other ship had no lights on. All of its windows were dark. It reminded him of a ghost ship from one of the novels he read as a young boy. The deck lights of the *Viking Trader* cast an eerie illumination on the bridge house of the other ship, where several frightened faces stared down from the windows at Captain Marzak. One person on the other ship was incredulously waving his hand to the side, as if to suggest that the *Viking Trader* should get out of the way. In slow motion, the Master watched as the reinforced metal bow of the container ship struck his vessel less than a hundred feet forward of where he was standing. To his surprise, the impact was not so much heard as felt. The *Viking Trader* immediately leaned backward, over to starboard, as the screeching of metal wafted in the heavy air. Like a duet, the container ship simultaneously heeled over to its opposite side. The two ships were now married together, doing a powerful tango above the still water's surface as the propulsion from the other ship continued to thrust forward.

Captain Marzak, who was knocked down by the collision, carefully rose on the angled deck and grabbed the handrails on the pilot table. He worked his way back to the bridge wing, not taking immediate notice that the helmsman was lying on the floor unconscious. The second mate was wiping blood off his own forehead after having struck the computer screen.

As Marzak opened the door to the wing and stepped outside on the platform, he could see the name of the container ship carved in a large brass plate on the side of the ship's house: *M/V Crazy Horse. Well*, thought the Captain, *I could not have given that ship a better name myself.* He reached the rail on the outermost edge of the wing and looked down at the damage to the two ships. Although it was difficult to see in the dark shadows, a thirty-foot gash had been created by the bulbous bow of the other ship, creasing, and eventually penetrating, the hull of the *Viking Trader*. It was right at the waterline. There was no doubt that his vessel was taking on some seawater, but it would have been a lot worse if the hull had been pierced further down.

The Master needed to find out how his engine crew was doing. As he was about to return to the bridge house, he stared in disbelief at the bottom of the *Crazy Horse*, which was now partly tilted into the air. Stuck to the dark-red metal sheets that covered the underwater part of the hull, and near the keel, was a huge, black, torpedo-shaped object more than sixty feet long. The bulbous front end of the object was caved in by the collision of the two ships. A small window at the very front of the cylinder was smeared on the inside with dark blood. A lifeless head was crushed against the glass surface.

The scene was like a pilot fish stuck to the bottom of a large shark, only both fish were now dead in the water.

Chapter 1
London

Joe Barrett cheerfully walked out the back doors of the Hilton Hotel on Pepys Street in the City of London, adjusted his unwanted and uncomfortable tie, and headed towards Fenchurch Street. It was early September and the weather was damp and brisk but it was still too early for an overcoat. He had finished a light breakfast in the coffee shop and was now walking in tandem with hundreds of workers who were on their way to the offices in the financial center of London. His tight, curly, black hair, just beginning to show streaks of white, had been trimmed just before he left New York. At the request of his girlfriend, Dalia, Joe finally broke down and bought an executive-looking blue suit and leather wingtip shoes for the impending meeting.

A maritime lawyer working in the midtown Manhattan law firm of Hooper & Kingsley, LLP., Joe traveled to Britain a couple of times a year because London remained the center for marine insurance and maritime law. A lot of his clients, or their underwriters, were within a ten-block radius of where he was standing. The Tower of London was over his right shoulder, the fluttering flags on its turrets popping in and out of view. He could also see the stone pylons of the beautiful Tower Bridge that crossed the Thames only a couple of blocks away. Traffic was at a standstill waiting to get over its narrow vehicle ramp as hundreds of pedestrians walked in both directions on the footpaths of the historic bridge bound for work.

Barrett was in no rush as his appointment with the East of England Protection and Indemnity insurance company was in another twenty minutes. He had lots of time. The marine insurance company had requested that Joe meet with them to discuss several cases he was handling in New York. In particular, they were focused on a lawsuit involving a large casualty caused by a ship that had caught on fire in the middle of the Atlantic Ocean while on its way to northern Europe. The East of England was not an ordinary insurance company. Since marine casualties could exceed the amount of insurance coverage available on the commercial markets, most of the major ship owners around the world formed mutual associations in which they agreed to protect each other from the financial risks of major accidents involving their ships. The majority of those mutual 'Clubs,' like the East of England, were located in the center of London.

Joe walked up Lloyds Avenue and checked his cell phone for messages. Dalia had sent a short text wishing him luck and telling him to enjoy the trip. She had recently taken the position of a paralegal in his office after providing critical assistance in a recent case involving a poisonous gas that was covertly shipped inside a sea container to New York by an Arab terrorist. Her Lebanese background and ability to speak Arabic had helped break that case. Joe grinned after reading the message but knew that their growing relationship was ultimately going to create a problem for the law firm, which did not encourage interoffice romances.

Ten minutes later, Barrett was walking into the World Ocean Marine building on Fenchurch with its towering lobby, dark granite stone walls, and brilliant white floors. Passing through fairly tough security, he took the "lift" up to the reception floor for East of London. After an unexpectedly long wait, he was greeted by Mike Graham, the manager of the club. Mike hurriedly led the way down the hall and into a small but elegant conference room. Two pots of tea and coffee, with some fancy biscuits, were already waiting on the expensive birchwood conference table. Joe turned and looked out the large floor-to-ceiling windows towards the east end of the city. He could see in the distance the distinctive office building dubbed the Gerkin because it looked so much like a pickle. It was a design that would never make it in New York.

"Good trip, I hope, Joe? You picked a nice week to be in London," Mike said as he offered the sidebar.

"Very nice flight, Mike. By the way, I followed your recommendation and had a bite to eat at the Sky Lounge when I got in last evening."

"That restaurant has great views of the city, and the food is not bad. Look, sorry for being a bit late in greeting you this morning, but I have been tied up with last week's collision of the *Viking Trader* and the *Crazy Horse* in the Channel."

Joe stirred some milk into his tea. He had known the manager of the club for more than a dozen years. In spite of the fact that Graham was approaching retirement, he still had more energy and bounce in his step than anyone else Joe knew. However, he now had the air of someone who was harried and distracted.

"Terrible accident," Joe said. "I've been reading about it in the trade papers. Half-dozen seamen killed and a lot of oil spilled into the Channel, which is now coming up on the beaches of France. I understand both vessels were considered constructive total losses. Not a good day in the annals of maritime transport or marine insurance, I guess."

"Yes," said the Brit as he took a seat across from Joe at the conference table. "But it is what you have not read in the press that really worries me."

"Sorry," replied Joe. "Come again?"

"This is extremely confidential, but the *Crazy Horse* is a Liberian flag vessel owned by the Hong Group in Korea. It's a family-run shipping company that keeps its ships in fairly good shape and hires competent seamen. The ship is less than a year old and it looks like it lost total auxiliary power due to some problem in the engine room about thirty minutes before the collision. No lights, no radar, no radio, no engine control, and no steering. We are still not sure why controls were lost, but the marine surveyors seem to think there may have been defective wiring in the engine room, which shorted out most of the electrical system. Unfortunately, the engines kept running and could not be shut down."

"So, that explains why the *Crazy Horse* could neither respond on the radio nor change speed or course," Barrett commented.

Mike Graham looked directly at him. "Yes, but it does not explain why the vessel continued to turn to starboard after the blackout. What you have not read is that they discovered a large submersible latched to the bottom of the *Crazy Horse*, which was apparently causing enough drag on the starboard side of that ship to continuously pull the vessel to the right, dragging it into the *Viking Trader's* lane. That's what caused the collision."

Joe's mouth opened but he did not know what to say. A couple of decades ago, there were rumors that drug cartels welded canisters and large tubes filled with drugs to the bottom of commercial freighters while in South American ports. The vessels then sailed to the United States or Europe. When they arrived, the drug cartels arranged to have divers secretly go into the water at night while the ships were tied up at berth. The waterproof canisters were removed from the ship bottom plates, and the divers dragged the barrels ashore. The drugs inside the canisters were sold on the street for millions of dollars. The Coast Guard eventually caught up with this trick. Random underwater inspections of vessels coming into the U.S. became a requirement of the Coast Guard. However, this was the first time that Joe had ever heard of a small submarine attaching itself to a cargo ship.

"That's unbelievable," Joe finally remarked. "What was in the submarine?"

Graham clicked the end of his pen a couple of times, and then said, "Mostly cocaine – tons of it. The consensus is that the sub attached itself to the *Crazy Horse* after she passed through the Panama Canal on her way to Europe."

"I must say that I am surprised because many governments are now checking the bottom of vessels when they berth."

"That's the scary part. This sub is self-powered and undetectable. It has a unique propulsion system. My engineers estimate it can travel underwater up to twenty-five knots for hundreds of miles. We think the sub leaves from some private location, dives underwater, and then attaches itself under a cargo ship while she is waiting to get into a port. Several powerful magnets are engaged from the top of the sub and it latches itself onto the bottom of the unsuspecting vessel. Having hitched a ride, the submersible can then travel long distances undetected. When it gets to where it is going, the sub releases itself and quietly goes off underwater to its own destination. Accomplishing its mission requires a lot of electronics on board the little craft."

"You mean the sub is manned? There was someone on board?" asked Joe.

"Yes, there was a single pilot, but he was killed in the collision. Interpol is trying to identify him."

"Any idea who might be behind the operation?"

"No idea. At first, we thought the pilot might be from the Far East, but it's difficult to say. He may be with one of the Columbian cartels. Anyway, the submersible was state-of-the-art and will change the whole game in maritime crime. Quite frankly, Joe, we are a lot more worried about those stealth subs being used to carry stowaways, terrorists, or even weapons. Government agencies are having heart attacks over this."

Joe thought for a second and then said, “Key to all of this is that someone designed, engineered, and built the sub. There is a lot of technology and investment there, and only a few builders would have access to the technology that you describe. Find the builder and you can cut off the proverbial head of that snake.”

Mike smiled and pushed a large pile of papers over towards Barrett. “Exactly what we thought. And that is the real reason why I asked you to fly over and see us. For obvious reasons, I didn't want to send any emails about the situation. Between our MI5 and your Homeland Security, the governments are putting a tight lid on this. However, with two cargo vessels being declared total losses, the insurance companies are out by more than two hundred million dollars just for the hulls, and twice that for the cargos. Add the death and personal injury claims, and this incident will cost the marine insurance market almost a billion dollars. We need to make sure it never happens again.”

Joe paused to think for a moment before adding, “It will cost a lot more than that if one of those mini-subs is used to blow up an anchorage of ships or a port.”

“Yes, the thought has occurred to us. Look at the file, Joe, and let us know what more you need.”

“Where is the sub now? I would like to start by looking at it.”

“It's at a British naval base in Portsmouth, although the base is not really used for subs. That was intentional. But there is a major research group located there. The commanding officer, Tom Heard, is a tough administrator, but as you Americans say, a ‘straight shooter.’ We'll arrange permission for you to inspect the sub and talk to the engineers looking at it.” Mike made some notes on a pad and then continued. “Where do you think you will go after inspecting the sub?”

“I need to talk to the Master of the *Crazy Horse*. See if we can pin down where and when the sub attached itself.”

"Done. We'll arrange for you to meet with the captain. Joe, you have to assure me that your office will keep this all very private and confidential. No room for mistakes. In fact, keep emails to a minimum. Refer to the sub as the 'Pilot Fish.'"

Joe put the file in his briefcase and stood. Nick wished him good luck and Joe headed back to the hotel. He had a lot of reading ahead of him.

Chapter 2
London

Upon entering his small room at the hotel, Joe threw the file on the bed and immediately pulled out his cell phone. He dialed the office and asked for Dalia. The phone rang only once before it was picked up. An excited and slightly out-of-breath female voice answered, "Joe, is everything OK? I didn't expect you to call until this evening." Then, there was a slight giggle. "Or maybe you just miss me."

Barrett laughed and responded that he had, of course, missed her. He really did wish that she had joined him for the trip, although things had unexpectedly changed with the new file.

"I just saw Mike Graham. We were given a major file to handle. Not the usual kind of case, and I can't go into a lot of details over the phone, but I need you to do some research for me. Start looking into shipyards that construct commercial or sport submarines, or any sort of robotic underwater craft. I'm not talking about toys; I'm talking about really advanced, serious stuff that is designed to hold passengers. Who is making those vehicles? Who are the leading experts in the field? Where are they sold? Who makes the power plants? If you see any unusual stories about submersibles, let me know."

"Unusual stories? Joe, I am not sure what you are talking about."

"Yeah. Sorry for being vague. We can talk more about it when I get home. For now, transfer me over to Captain Ken." The captain was his senior paralegal, an ex-Master of cargo ships, whose career came to a grinding halt when his assigned vessel stranded on some rocks owing to a mistake by his Third Mate while the Captain was sleeping. But the buck always stops with the Master, and Ken, a smart, athletic, good-looking man in his early fifties, was summarily dismissed by the steamship line. By chance, he was picked up by the law firm of Hooper & Kingsley when they were looking for a maritime expert to assist at a trial. Since then, Ken had become an invaluable member of Joe's team and provided the gritty details of marine science and practice that Joe often needed to succeed in his cases.

"Are you still coming home Friday?" asked Dalia.

"That may be messed up now. After I talk with Captain Ken, I'll have a better idea. But I expect I may have to stay here another two or three days."

"Bet that means another week. Well, I am glad you got the new case and I'll be here when you get back home. Let me transfer you over to Ken."

Joe waited a few more seconds and then he heard Captain Ken say hello. "Ken, I need you on the first flight out to London. We have a major investigation to do. Graham has us working on a confidential job and I need your experience on this one."

There was a slight delay as Ken could be heard typing at his computer keyboard. "There's a BA flight at eleven tonight. Computer says there are seats on board. I'll be at the hotel by noon tomorrow. What do I need to bring?" Joe and Captain Ken spent the next fifteen minutes going over what materials needed to be brought to England. Joe hung up the phone and put the pile of documents on the small study desk in the room. He turned on the overhead light, pulled a beer out of the small fridge, and loosened his tie. Joe began from the top of the file that Graham had handed him and made handwritten notes on his yellow legal pad. Five hours later, he was several inches into the documents.

Chapter 3
Seoul

The dim glow from an expensive brass lamp left a circular glow across the beautiful patina of the ancient mahogany desk in Wook Hong's office, located in the Jongo District, a palace quarter in the heart of Seoul. The director of Hong Lines, known locally as HGI, was the oldest member of a powerful family cartel whose ancestors could be traced back for centuries. Wook was working late, which was normal. What was not normal was the lithe and shadowy figure in the far corner of his immense office, who was sitting silently on an eighteenth-century French wing chair. The man was dressed entirely in black with rubber sole shoes and wearing a hood that was pulled back over his long slick hair. Wook, who was portly and short, tried to put on the air of someone who was in command and demanded respect. In truth, he was absolutely frightened. He held out his right hand, which was showing signs of tremors in the fingers.

"Mr. Director," the figure in the shadow said in an ice-cold breath, "my principals are not happy. You lost their submersible and its contents. That cost them nearly one hundred million dollars, about the same cost as a missile. Very, very bad for the Hong family."

Wook did not like threats, and he did not like this messenger. However, he was even more frightened of the messenger's boss. He admitted that it was a serious mistake to have gotten into a relationship with the employer but it was a necessary evil, given the circumstances.

Chapter 3

"You tell your boss that the Hong family did not intentionally destroy the sub or its contents. The collision was unavoidable and certainly not foreseen. The Hong family has also suffered hundreds of millions of dollars of losses from the destruction of its new container ship and the death of some of the crew." Wook turned to sit in his stuffed leather chair. "I told you before that you should have two pilots on board every sub, so there is a backup in the event of an emergency. And how many times have I told your boss that the subs must be secured underneath the rear of the cargo ship? But your experts insisted the submersibles be latched up forward near the bow. They claimed that would make it easier for the sub to get away if the cargo vessel was stopped. Well, it was stopped. Stopped dead in the ocean by a head-on collision. The haste and incompetence of your boss is what has caused all these problems."

"My employer does not see it that way. And if this problem is not corrected, he will bring down your company, then your family, and then you."

"What does he expect me to do?" asked Hong, who was beginning to tire of the threats by the messenger. It was bad enough that his company had several governments and their secret services asking questions, as well as the International Maritime Organization, Interpol, the Korean Maritime Commission, the Panamanian Flag Registry, and his own insurance company. Wook was not deeply concerned about those organizations finding anything – even the Captain of the *Crazy Horse* had no idea about the sub. But the director of Hong Shipping was worried that someone would find out about the financial problems his company had been suffering in the weak commercial market. To cover the millions of dollars in losses over the past two years, Wook had borrowed heavily from this devil's boss to keep the company running. If Hong's own banks had any wind of the financial problems, they would start calling in their substantial loans. There were also a few Korean government ministers who were sniffing around, concerned about the overall health of the country's entire maritime industry after one of the largest container carriers in the world, based in Korea, had recently filed for global bankruptcy.

"What does your boss expect me to do?" Wook asked once more.

"Get the submersible back, or destroy it."

"Why? The whole front end was destroyed by the collision. Your pilot died. The craft was seized by the British Navy. The drugs inside have certainly been seized. You go get it!"

There was an almost imperceptible flicker of the hand in the shadow, followed by a faint whistle and a solid thump. Buried in the beautiful, hand-polished wood surface of the director's desk, only two inches from the trembling right hand, was a small, shiny metal star, its razor-sharp tips reflecting the light from the overhead lamp. It was a shuriken, a nasty little weapon, often seen in ninja movies on late-night television being thrown one after another and somehow deflected by the hero. In reality, they were so small and fast that it was nearly impossible to stop them from embedding in the flesh. The look on the director's face was pure shock, not just from the fact that he could have suffered damage to his hand, but more importantly that his five-hundred-year-old antique desk had been permanently marred.

"Now that I have your full attention," said the messenger in a quiet voice, "you will get the submersible back or destroy it. Our information is that it is lying at the Portsmouth Naval Base."

"How?"

"Use your considerable influence and assets to get it back. Otherwise, another of your precious cargo ships may suffer a similar fate." With that, the messenger arose from the chair and walked to the back of the room and exited through the secret opening in the wall.

Wook carefully wiggled the sharp star until it finally came out of the wood, leaving a permanent gash in the desktop. The old man sat at his chair, thought for a few moments, and then picked up the phone. He recognized that there were very few options left open to him.

Chapter 4
Portsmouth

The hotel hostess, dressed properly in a severe black dress and white blouse, with black stockings, brought in a new tray of snacks. She carefully set the platter down on the conference room table where Joe Barrett and Captain Ken were reviewing materials from the East of England. She smiled with more than a hint of attraction towards Joe and asked if he would mind if she moved a few papers on the desk so as to move the tray to the center. Joe mumbled his approval without moving his eyes from the spreadsheet in front of him. The hostess gave a pout and asked, "Will there be anything else?" She then glided out of the room. Ken looked over towards Joe and laughed, "It's amazing how you can charm women even when you are not trying."

"Don't ever repeat that to Dalia or I'm a dead man," responded Barrett, his eyes still glued to the document in front of him. "Did you notice that the last port of call for the *Crazy Horse* was Pusan, Korea? She went all the way across the Pacific Ocean, through the Panama Canal, and was headed to Rotterdam when the accident occurred. That's one hell of a long voyage. She didn't even stop for fuel."

Ken looked over Joe's shoulder at the sheet. "The vessel's manifest indicates most of the cargo was destined for Northern Europe, so I am not surprised at the length of the trip, but there were some containers destined for Piraeus and Alexandria. Funny that the ship didn't proceed westbound from Korea and come through the Suez Canal. That would have been a shorter trip and cost the shipowner less money. The companies I worked for watched every penny and would never have taken the more expensive route."

Joe made some notes in the margin of the next document, and then looked out the small window towards a grey and cloudy sky. "What do we know about Hong Lines, the owner of the *Crazy Horse*? I recall from the trade journals that they own over a hundred ships and are having several more built. Company has been around for about sixty years. Wook Hong is in charge, but there is talk that, at his age, he cannot lead much longer. He has two sons; one was educated at Columbia University. The family is very secretive about their holdings."

"Nothing unusual there. That's pretty common with a lot of family-owned steamship lines around the world."

"Of course. But the sixty-four dollar question is whether Hong Shipping knew they had a submarine stuck to the bottom of their ship, or if they were just a victim?"

Ken cleared his throat, sat back, and reflected. "Well, we know that the Captain of the *Crazy Horse* adamantly told the Royal Navy that he was unaware of the sub, and he seems to have been pretty well grilled on the subject. Of course, that does not mean that old man Hong did not know about the Pilot Fish. But I am at a loss to understand what benefit Hong Lines would have gotten out of the arrangement. Shipping lines today face huge penalties and criminal sanctions if they allow drugs to get on their ships. The fines can run into the millions of dollars. And the vessel can be blacklisted from being allowed back into critical ports or even the entire country. The crew can be arrested if the authorities find drugs. My contacts in the U.S. Coast Guard tell me that Hong Lines has a pretty good reputation for preventing drugs from being loaded on their ships. You would think that if they don't want drugs inside their ships, they don't want drugs under their ship."

"You're probably right, but I think we ought to get Dalia and Tim Murphy to start doing some serious research on the company." Tim Murphy was the senior associate working under Joe. He had been with Hooper & Kingsley for nearly six years after having graduated near the top of his class from New York University law school.

As Captain Ken called New York regarding the research needed on Hong Lines, Joe opened a thin blue folder and reviewed the few documents that were obtained from the Royal Navy investigators. Some of it was redacted with a black marker pen. There was only one photo showing the damaged submarine inside a storage warehouse. The lighting was poor, but the photograph indicated that the vessel was not homemade. The craft was obviously fabricated with some kind of advanced material. The welding work and joints were all very high grade. The surface of the craft appeared to be coated with some sort of seamless rubber paint, perhaps to keep down noise and avoid anyone tracking the submersible. There were two sets of retracting hydroplanes on each side of the sub, which presumably provided stability when the craft was under its own propulsion. The tail fins had a delicate curve as the thin wings moved aft. They reminded Joe of the assembly on the deadly bombs dropped out of the belly of aircrafts in World War II movies. A joint at the base of the tail indicated that the fins could be moved so as to control movement up, down, left, and right. One of the most unusual structures on the sub were the eight pods, the size of dinner plates, mounted in two rows along the top surface. They apparently provided the magnetic grip to the steel hull of the *Crazy Horse*.

Joe also noted that there were no propellers on the sub in the picture. Instead, there were two aggressive wide-mouth ducts near the bow that looked like giant vacuum cleaner attachments. Both of them had suffered damage from the crushing. There were four similar, albeit larger, ducts near the tail. Whoever had built this submersible had obviously put a lot of money and engineering into it. Indeed, to Joe, the craft seemed a little out of Star Wars, and a bit extravagant for the drug trade.

Joe suddenly realized there was another unusual feature. "Ken, if we assume that this submersible was latched onto the *Crazy Horse* as it exited the Panama Canal into the Gulf of Mexico, there must have been over ten days of air that the sub provided the pilot while the vessel was underwater. Isn't that a hell of a lot of air for something that is only about sixty feet long?"

"Got to admit, it sounds amazing to me. Snorkel tubes could not be used by the sub to bring in surface air because it was attached too far underneath the container ship. Probably means that the vehicle was constructed with a scrubber system for the atmosphere inside the sub. I suspect she has some oxygen tanks in the event of an emergency. That's pretty sophisticated stuff. Almost sounds military to me."

"Exactly what I was thinking. I believe it's time we drive down to Portsmouth and talk to the engineers on the base. Besides, I'm getting hungry and I know the perfect place for lunch. But you better drive; I'll get us killed at the first roundabout with the left-side driving."

Captain Ken seemed very comfortable at the wheel of the four-door, grey-colored Opel sedan as they drove on the M3 highway towards the picturesque town of Portsmouth. The town is located on the south coast of England about seventy-five miles southwest of London, and next to Southampton. It is a city best known to Americans as the place from where the *Titanic* departed on her fateful voyage in 1912. The small engine whined, but the car made good speed as they kept up with relatively light traffic. Joe spotted the sign for New Forest, where the M3 joined the M27, and directed Ken to exit. The New Forest National Park was one of the largest remaining tracts of unenclosed forest and pasture land in

England, lying just west of Southampton. Home to many species of wild animals, including wild boar and the small barking deer, it was declared a royal forest by William the Conqueror in 1079, and thereafter became a source of oak for the Royal Navy.

After driving a few miles under canopies of tall oaks and pines, with wild horses feeding on the tall grass, the Opel crossed the old stone bridge at Fordingbridge, just on the edge of New Forest. Ken carefully turned the car into the small gravel parking lot of the George Inn, a beautiful eighteenth-century pub set on the banks of the dark-blue River Avon. The whitewashed stone walls and the redbrown slate roof with its towering chimney were right out of a Disney movie. The Inn was fairly empty as it was still not noontime. Joe asked for a table out on the terrace overlooking the swift-running stream. The waiter, a fresh-faced kid who had recently graduated high school, handed them the menus. Joe chuckled when he read the warning that all of the game on the menu was "locally shot and may contain pieces of shot. Please be careful." They both enjoyed sipping from a somewhat chilled half pint of "Ringwood's Best," a local bitter ale, while their orders for wild mushroom, crispy pork belly, and pan-roasted duck were being prepared.

"I thought you were going to bring Dalia along on this trip," said Ken, looking at the faint line of suds in his glass. "No problems between you two, I hope?"

"No problems, I assure you. Just that I did not think the firm would like two employees knowingly fraternizing with one another, and picking up the travel expenses as well."

"Well, it's not like anyone is not aware of your relationship with Dalia, and frankly, I think everyone approves. I might add that she has calmed you down a bit, and meanwhile, the firm gets one hell of a good paralegal as well."

"Everyone can acknowledge our relationship, but it still borders on a violation of the firm rule against nepotism. I just don't want Dalia to get hurt by the situation, especially since she is so happy with the job and making the extra income."

"Has anyone said anything negative to you, Joe?"

"Not really, but I keep thinking that old man McDonald keeps giving me the evil eye." Joe was referring to Alistair J. McDonald, the 76-year-old crusty and fastidious managing partner of the firm, who rarely saw eye-to-eye with Joe.

"Well," Ken replied with a hearty laugh, "I guess that proves my point. Nine months ago, you would never have cared about firm rules, much less about McDonald. Dalia has put a charm on you."

Joe was silent and continued looking out at the fast-moving currents in the river. Swans and ducks floated effortlessly on the surface of the water, seemingly enjoying the free ride. "Fact of the matter, Ken, is that I am thinking of proposing to her, and I am frightened that will end with one of us having to leave the firm. I think I am pretty clever in finding solutions to most problems, but this one may be hopeless."

"I think you are over-thinking this, Joe. The firm knows the four of us are a very valuable team, and we bring in a lot of revenue and reputation to the firm. I don't think they would want to break that up. My humble suggestion would be for you to meet with McDonald and have a talk. He may be more reasonable than you think." As the captain finished his comments, the platters of food arrived. The aroma was intoxicating and each of the plates had been garnished with fresh local vegetables and wild rice. Both men did not waste another second and dove into their dishes with gusto. After a little more than an hour, and another pint of ale, the two Americans were looking stuffed and satisfied.

"Who says the British can't cook?" Ken commented as he wiped his lips with a napkin to remove the last drops of the wonderful orange sauce basted onto the crispy duck. "The poor driver of that Pilot Fish doesn't know what he missed. He was probably eating beef jerky for weeks before the collision."

"Actually," said Joe, "that's a good question. What did he eat and drink? Maybe the leftover food onboard the sub will give us an idea of where he came from, or at least what port he started from. And having said that, I think we need to get back on the road. We have a meeting with the Royal Commander in less than an hour. I don't think he is going to be enthusiastic about seeing two Americans from a law firm." Joe paid the bill and the two men left the inn. Less than five minutes later, they were back on the highway headed towards Portsmouth.

Her Majesty's Naval Base in Portsmouth was one of three naval bases in the United Kingdom. It was home to one of the oldest dry docks in the world, as well as being the headquarters for two-thirds of the Royal Navy's surface fleet. While there were no submarines assigned to the base, visitors could tour a submarine museum and several historic vessels, including the HMS Victory and the HMS Warrior. Ken carefully wound himself around the narrow cobblestone streets and past many of the administrative buildings. He then drove along the brick walls of Priddy's Hard Gosport, a part of Portsmouth's historic dockyard. Joe Barrett had been specifically instructed not to stop at any of the official buildings at the Royal base. Rather, they were to go directly to Boathouse Number 4, a building constructed just before 1940. It stood out from the other eighteenth-century brick buildings because it was made out of corrugated metal with a sawtooth roof. The boathouse had been turned into a museum for skills training and well known for its exhibition of the 'forgotten craft,' the small boats which were the backbone of the Royal Navy for centuries.

Ken followed the signs along the waterfront, turned through the Victory Gate, which was built in 1711, and slowly headed down Main Road. On the left, moored to a long dock, which stretched into the harbor, was the magnificent battleship, *HMS Warrior,* which had been mothballed since World War II. On the other side of the pier was another war relic, a small, grey PT boat that looked in perfect condition. At the head of the dock was the parking lot for Boat House 4. The building sat right at the water's edge of Portsmouth Harbor. Joe, dressed in jeans with a navy blue blazer and pinstripe cotton shirt, walked along the gravel path to the front door. Ken followed behind carrying a large briefcase filled with the documents provided by the client.

A guard, dressed in a dark blue uniform with a brimmed hat and polished boots, greeted them at the door. Joe was a little surprised as he understood the exhibition was free and required no tickets. The guard, who had apparently been alerted to intercept both Joe and Ken, politely directed them to the back of the building and the "college" entrance. The two Americans kept to the path and slowly worked their way around to the back of the building. Halfway around the structure, they found a single door, over which hung the sign "Highbury College." Joe quickly descended several steps in front of the door and gave a firm rap with his knuckles. To his surprise, the door was not made of tin, as it appeared, but was rather fabricated of some heavy metal that provided serious protection. A CCTV camera rotated on the wall above. Its lens was focused on the two men. A voice from a speaker somewhere under the camera instructed the Americans to turn completely around and then inquired if they were carrying any arms. Both Joe and Ken, staring back at the black lens, shook their heads and firmly said "no." A click was heard and the thick door quietly opened outwards. The hidden voice told the two men to step lively into the doorway. As soon as they cleared the threshold, another click was heard and the heavy door remotely closed behind them, followed by the sound of a thud as a solid lock snapped into place.

A large mirrored window lined one wall in the small vestibule while the other three walls were painted bright white. Several strong halogen lamps shone down from the ceiling making Joe feel very uncomfortable. A voice finally came over a speaker hidden in the wall instructing the men to face the mirrored window. They immediately did so and Joe removed his worn baseball cap. The androgynous voice then asked them to state their names and the purpose of their visit.

"I'm Joe Barrett, an attorney from New York with the firm of Hooper & Kingsley. This is my associate, Ken Libby. Our client is the East of England. They have asked us to investigate an incident involving the vessel *Crazy Horse*. I was told by Mike Graham of the Club that we should speak with Commanding Officer Tom Heard, and that he has agreed to allow us an examination of the craft." Joe's comment was met with silence. Some shuffling could be heard behind the walls, but no voices. After about three minutes, a door, cleverly built into the far side of the vestibule, slowly opened. Ken picked up the briefcase and the two men headed through the door.

The other side was very industrial. Everything seemed to be made out of concrete, with overhead pipes and ventilation ducts exposed along the high ceiling. Steel girders seemed to run in all directions. Rows of long modern LED lamps hung from steel straps on the ceiling and provided sufficient lighting, albeit in hospital style. Joe was certain he had seen the same set design in a *Dr. Who* series. A number of people wearing lab coats scurried about, some in groups of two or three, talking in hushed tones. Joe wisely decided not to move beyond the security room door until greeted. Almost immediately, a tall, confident man with short wavy blond hair, probably in his mid-fifties, walked into view. He was dressed in a stiff white shirt, black tie, and a dark black uniform with the Royal Navy insignia patches on his sleeve and cap. Next to him stood a very attractive lady in her early thirties. She was red-headed with light freckles and light blue eyes, wearing a formal black skirt and jacket with a starched blouse and a white cap. She carried a couple of folders under her right arm and had a very serious look on her face. Still, Joe had the impression they had gotten the "once-over" from the young lady officer.

"I am Commander Heard, Mr. Barrett. Glad to make your acquaintance. Nick said a lot of good things about you, even if you are a Yank." Heard smiled and held out his hand. "And this is my assistant, Yeoman Vivian Fox. A bit serious, but she is very good at her job." The commander smiled again before facing Ken with a quizzical look. Joe spoke up. "This is Captain Ken Libby, my legal assistant. He holds a Master's license and sailed for several years before coming ashore."

The commander looked Ken in the eyes and gave another firm handshake. "Actually, Captain, I am well aware of the misfortune that your career at sea encountered. At one time, I studied your case for a paper I gave on the risks and responsibilities that comes with being a ship's Master. I cited you as an example of what our navies and merchant marine need today: officers who acknowledge that they are responsible for what occurs under their command. The fact is that both the man at the top and the man who did the wrong need to face consequences when things go wrong at sea. It's tough, but when you are a thousand miles at sea, and lives are at stake, there is no time for democracy to rule." Commander Heard paused and then commented, "However, I must say that I do not think that your employer recognized the sacrifices you made or the good judgment you exercised after the event. Very bad luck." Once again, he shook Ken's hand, and then pointed the men to a glass-enclosed conference room at the end of the hall.

As they followed the tall commander, Joe looked over and saw that Captain Ken was standing up straight and rigid. He had obviously taken the Brit's comments to heart. Ken had been very quiet about the incident for the past six years. His vessel grounded because of an error by a junior officer on watch who misread the buoys going out of the port of Boston. Captain Ken was in his cabin, off duty, and asleep. The ship went aground on some rocks and suffered a hole in her hull that pierced a tank where fuel oil was stored. The oil that spilled out of the vessel landed on the coastline of Massachusetts. The beaches in the Cape Cod area were closed for weeks. Captain Ken Libby's name and picture were all over the press. However, the fact was that he had significantly reduced the potential for a much larger spill by forcing the vessel further up on the shoal after the grounding and transferring ballast to the opposite side. The result was the vessel listed, causing the side with the gash to rise up into the air, and that significantly stemmed the gush of oil leaking out of the ship.

The company felt pressured into "releasing" Ken given the public outrage over the spill, even though the Coast Guard investigation found that Captain Libby had personally done nothing wrong. The Coast Guard panel also concluded that his actions after the tank was punctured probably reduced by half the amount of oil that could have polluted the shoreline. Still, Captain Ken had repeatedly told the press and the Coast Guard that, as the Master of the ship, he had to take ultimate responsibility for the error by his junior officer. Ken personally apologized to those impacted by the oil slick along the shoreline, including fisherman, yachtsman, and homeowners. Fortunately, because the grounding was in late November, the water was relatively cold. The oil slick was easier to contain and most of it was swept up. But the public relations damage was more permanent. It was nearly a year before Captain Ken Libby was able to find a job with the law firm of Hooper & Kingsley.

After everyone was seated in the conference room, Commander Tom Heard instructed Yeoman Fox to hand over folders that were marked "unclassified." The contents included additional photos of the submarine, some of which showed details of the interior of the vessel. There were also some laboratory reports showing a spectral analysis of the hull, the autopsy of the pilot, a measurement of the vehicle's dimensions, and technical details of the propulsion system. Joe and Ken went slowly through the documents while the British officers watched. Finally, Joe looked up, adjusted his seating and said, "It looks like it was newly built, most likely the Far East, and quite advanced in respect to its propulsion, controls, communication, and navigation systems. However, I don't see any conclusions as to who built it or who operated it."

The commander smiled, and then indicated to Ms. Fox that it was time to retrieve the materials from the two gentlemen. "Let's just say that we have our suspicions, and so does your government, but we are not ready to put that into print for right now."

"Actually, Joe," interrupted Captain Ken, "I believe the reason why our governments are most worried about this submersible is because it is partly fabricated from a man-made material found in ballistic missiles. Moreover, the propulsion system is out of the future, a magnetic drive that uses neodyminium-iron-boron permanent magnets that create an induced magnetic force for torque transfer. The result is no vibration, no noise, and increased efficiency – very hard for even military sonar to detect. I suspect our own navies are experimenting with this stuff and wish they had it in their fleet. In short, it's a phantom ship."

Commander Heard looked hard at Captain Ken and then gave a short chuckle. "I forgot, you had advanced degrees in engineering as well. Very good, Captain. We did not think most people would pick up on those points. However, while you may freely speak about those technical details in this building, I trust that outside of this building you will show the same professionalism and confidences that I credited you with in my thesis." With a very serious look, the commander added, "There are a lot more ships and lives involved now."

The officer stood up at the table and looked at his guests. "Alright, time to go see the phantom. Yeoman Fox will take you to the testing tank that lies in the back of Boat House Number 4. It is actually used by Highbury College to test hull designs. We felt this building is the most secure place to test the craft and at the same time have access to the scientists who are qualified for this research. You will have to excuse me now as I must head back to my office. Thank you, gentlemen. I trust we will have your strict confidence on this whole matter." With that, the commander shook hands once more and headed back down the concrete corridor.

"Gentlemen," Ms. Fox said in a deadly serious tone as the door to the room closed. "You are required to wear these badges at all times. You will not remove any materials or papers from this facility, as well as any photos you take must be approved by us. You will not stray away from the craft and any questions you have for the staff must be asked in my presence. Oh, and the commander's request that everything remain confidential and secret must actually be acknowledged on our legal forms, which I have prepared. Just sign the bottom of each page." She handed Joe a pen and quickly shifted through the pages for his initials without really giving him a chance to read the contents. Joe recalled that it was the British who invented drawing and quartering their enemies, so there was not much point in reading the fine print. But what happened to that elusive smile he thought the striking red-headed Yeoman had shown them as they entered the underground fortress? Joe suddenly realized that he miscalculated the trajectory of that initial flirtation. It was apparently directed to Captain Ken, who was standing behind Joe. Fox guided Ken slowly through each of the pages, and after brushing a couple of strands of her silky hair off her forehead, sweetly took the pen back from Ken's hand. *Well,* thought Joe, *that is a life-saver. One less yeoman I have to explain to Dalia.*

Fox led them through a series of corridors and opened several doors with her electronic badge. There were no guards in the hallways, but the dozens of pot-sized black bubbles that dotted the ceilings made it clear that there was video surveillance everywhere. The last door opened into a large room that immediately stung Joe's nostrils with the smell of chlorine. The entire length of the room was taken up by a huge pool, which was more accurately called a model basin. Along each side of the pool ran metal rails with pendant arms that could be attached to scale hull models. The large model boats would be dragged by the mechanical arms through the pool at various speeds to determine the efficiency and seaworthiness of the design. The one oddity that Joe noted about this tank was that it was "L" shaped, and extended beyond the building's back wall into Portsmouth bay so that vessels could be towed from the harbor into the tank and tested inside the building. The wall separating the pool from the bay was similar to a garage door but constructed of hundreds of opaque glass panes. The wall had been lifted slightly on its track by three or four feet. Through the opening, Joe spotted the pier where the *HMS Warrior* battleship was berthed, as well as the grey PT boat. Hundreds of tourists were lined up to go onboard the old battleship.

Parked inside the shed at the far end of the pool was the Pilot Fish, with its dark and slick surface bobbing on the surface of the water. The sub's bow was still crushed-in, much like the front end of a car when it hits a stone wall at high speed, but amazingly, it was still watertight in spite of the damage. The top surface was unusually flat, apparently to accommodate the sub's tight fit to the bottom of its victim ship. Eight pods, less than a half-foot tall, could be seen protruding from the top surface, four on each side, all equally spaced. The yeoman explained that each pod was equipped with a powerful electromagnet, which explained how the sub had attached itself to the *Viking Trader*.

Captain Ken's eye focused on four wide-mouth ducts built into the tapered back end of the submersible. He assumed these ports were designed to blast streams of water behind the sub and thereby thrust the vessel forward. It reminded him of the add-on tailpipes his high school friends would put on a worn-out Dodge to give the impression there was a high powered engine in the car.

Near the bow, two scoops were aimed forward. There was no standard screw-type propeller on the sub; obviously, seawater was sucked in through the two scoops mounted on the bow. The water then ran through tubes inside the sub, where it was then injected into the magnetic drive. The magneto drive expelled the compressed water through the four ducts at the tail with the force of a small jet engine, albeit without the noise. The result was quiet efficiency and no propeller cavitation. Steering was accomplished by simply changing the aim of the exhaust pipes. Marveling at the unique technology, Captain Ken lifted his camera with the telescopic lens from his shoulder strap to take a picture of the ports. The soft but firm hand of Yeoman Fox pressed down on the camera, and with her index finger, she wagged a naughty no. Ken was actually embarrassed.

The hatch cover for the sub was already in the open position so they climbed down the short vertical ladder. The interior was surprisingly bright, with light emitting from behind panels on both the walls and ceiling. Joe noticed that all the surfaces of the sub's interior, from ceiling to floor, were made out of a soft material. Capt. Ken saw the look on Joe's face and simply responded, "For sound and temperature insulation. Very effective and very expensive."

Chapter 4

The inside of the sub was a little over six feet in height, just enough so that Joe could stand up straight, although he instinctively wanted to bend over. It was a cavernous room that reminded Joe of an empty warehouse. Looking forward, the crushed bridge was heavily damaged. The pilot seat, looking more like a movie theater recliner, was damaged from the blow of the crumpled skin of the craft. Some instrumentation in the mangled wreckage could be identified, including the remains of a very large and cracked video monitor, which had been mounted above the narrow front window. The crew probably relied more on the monitor for infra-red images and sonar when underwater. It would be too dark in the murky Atlantic to see much through a window, especially while parked under the shadow of a ship's hull.

"I see there is a small galley for cooking food and a head against the rear bulkhead, but I don't see any engine equipment or fresh air processors," remarked Joe, who kept stooping over inside the sub.

"Probably on a deck underneath this one. It would keep the center of gravity low for the craft, which is essential to maintain stability. What I can't figure out is why all this empty space, even if it's for transporting drugs? Why build a truck when a small SUV would have done the trick?" Ken pulled out a flashlight and looked at Yeoman Fox for approval to turn it on. She gave a hint of a smile, and Ken then aimed the powerful beam on the floor. He spotted a seam about ten feet long that ran down the middle of the floor in the cargo area.

"Hello, what is this? A crack in the middle of the ship?" asked Joe.

Ken quickly responded, "No. It's a seam. Both sides of the floor swing down and out, allowing whatever is inside the cargo compartment to fall to the bottom of the sea. Water doesn't come into the craft because of the air pressure."

Joe was silent for a moment and then said, "Pretty strange, but I guess that is how they deliver the drugs. Maybe they are carried in watertight canisters. Here, take a look."

Ensign Fox walked up to the damaged pilot chair and pointed to a pod attached to the arm of the chair. Although parts of it were bent and mangled, the pod had rows of buttons, levers, and controls. Joe watched as she pressed a red button at the top, and then shifted her grip to a small lever near the base of the panel. She slowly shifted the lever to right, like a manual transmission on an old sports car, and then pulled back slowly on the lever. Joe immediately heard machinery under the deck flooring come to life. As he turned, he could see each side of the floor in the middle of the room separate at the seam. The floor panels slowly rotated downwards, somehow disappearing into the sidewall. A ten-by-ten-foot pool of water, with small ripples lapping over the edge, appeared in front of him. Fox then closed the hatch in the floor.

"That was fun," Joe remarked.

Ken then aimed the light along the wall where it met the floor. "I still can't find the hatch to access the engines. Wait a second, what have we got here?" He walked along the left-side wall to the middle of the cargo hold. He bent over and picked up something with a pair of tweezers from his shirt pocket. Ms. Fox, who stood next to him, pointed out that he was not to touch the object he just removed as it could be critical evidence. Ken held it up in the air to examine it in the light from one of the ceiling lamps. He twisted the small piece of paper. "It's a corner of a $100 bill!"

Ms. Fox looked at the edge of paper held between the tweezers' blades. She then asked Ken not to let the small piece of paper go until she got an evidence pouch. Without a moment's hesitation, the captain reached into a side pocket of his briefcase with his one free hand and produced a clear, plastic, sealable bag used for taking evidence. For the first time, Yeoman Fox revealed signs of a smile on her face. Ken noticed that her red lips competed with her short red hair, which gave her a pixie-like look. She held the bag wide open while Ken carefully inserted the small piece of paper money. The British officer then closed the bag and sealed it. She looked at Ken and then softly stated, "Thank you, Captain Libby. We found evidence of U.S. currency in two other places in the sub."

Joe thought for a second and then commented, "I don't think they were taking drugs and money in the same direction. I suspect the money was the payoff for the drugs that were delivered. They had already carried currency before this voyage when its cargo of cocaine ended in a collision. Carrying the money in the submersible would have made it impossible to trace the movement of the funds. No laundering was required. Ingenious."

"Joe, you could be right, but it still doesn't explain why all this empty space is required. This sub was designed for more than drugs and money. I just can't put my finger on it."

Yeoman Fox looked at Captain Ken and interjected, "The volume of space has been bothering our people as well. We are uncertain what this craft was designed to transport, but it could be fairly large and heavy – enough to fill at least one sea containers. Would you gentlemen like to speak to our head of research back in the lab?" Ms. Fox asked.

"Yes, thank you. I think we have seen enough here." Joe then followed the distinct redhead back up the straight ladder and onto the decking around the pool. She led them through a door into a small theater room where Dr. George Locke was in deep conversation with two lab technicians. He looked up and waived the visitors over to a table where he was standing. In the center of the table was a three-foot model of the submersible sitting on a stand. Captain Ken immediately bent over and looked at the detail of the replica.

"Amazing what lasers and 3D printers can do, isn't it?" said Dr. Locke. His salt-and-pepper beard and oversized, black-frame glasses gave him the look of a rogue scientist from some science fiction movie. The yeoman introduced the two Americans and excused herself to take an important call. Dr. Locke explained that he was the lead scientist assigned by the British government to examine the craft. While there was a lot of very advanced technology in the vessel, they had not been able to pinpoint where it was manufactured. "My best guess is maybe Korea or Japan. The materials and joinery are of an exceptional quality, and where there is welding, it is extremely well done. That is one of the reasons why we have focused on those two countries. They have the talent from their excellent shipyards to produce this kind of an advanced craft. We also found a couple of electronic components that were manufactured in Korea on the ship. The only other option would be a foreign government research lab, but none of the governments we contacted are acknowledging this submersible."

Joe looked more carefully at the detailed model and then asked, "Have you figured out why it was built? Seems to us that the sub is overkill for just carrying drugs or money. It must have been designed with something else in mind."

"We agree. But we haven't figured that out yet. Whatever it was designed to carry could weigh about fifty tons, or take up about three thousand cubic feet."

"Were there any weapons built into the craft?" asked Captain Libby.

"None that we could find, but given the power system, advanced electronics, and guidance system, there is nothing that would prevent some high-end weapon from being installed. Frankly, there was not a lot of wear and tear on the sub. We estimate it had only been used two or three times before the collision."

"Any idea how fast and far she could travel?" Ken inquired.

"Our estimate has increased. It now looks like she could do about thirty knots underwater with the magneto drive and probably had a range of about five hundred miles. However, what is most impressive is that the craft was designed to stay underwater for more than a month, recycling the air and making freshwater out of seawater." The scientist then chuckled before adding, "But it looks like the driver was living on cans of spam, salmon, and tuna fish. That would have brought me to the surface a lot sooner."

"What brand was the tuna fish?" Joe asked. "I'm being serious. Maybe it can help identify the country where the sub was operated from."

"No apology for the question. We thought the same thing. There were a couple of cans from China; the rest were Bumble Bee, but the kind sold in South America. We have pretty much ruled out the Chinese because we don't believe they have the technical expertise in their commercial shipyards to do this kind of work. Maybe they can do it in the government dungeons, but our intelligence suggests the Chinese were not behind this. In any event, they would not go to the trouble of making this craft for the purposes of selling drugs."

Ken then asked, "What do you intend to do with the sub?"

"Probably take it for a drive. We are planning to repair the critical instruments and install a new video monitor. The nose does not leak even though it has been crushed. Amazing. We would like to see how well the magnetic drive really works and get a better idea of her top speed and maneuverability. Subject to checking in with Yeoman Fox, you are welcome to come and watch. Now gentlemen, if there is nothing further to add, I really must attend a meeting with my colleagues."

Dr. Locke then packed up some materials on the desk and briskly headed off towards the back of the theater. The yeoman appeared on cue and Joe and Ken headed back to their car. Ken asked Ms. Fox if they could watch the sea trial of the sub in two days, as Dr. Locke mentioned. She was obviously pleased that Ken would be returning and confirmed that she would make the arrangements.

As Ken maneuvered the Opel out of the parking lot, the shadow of a figure standing behind a clump of trees across the street peered around a tree trunk and took a series of photos of Boathouse Number 4 with a high-powered Nikon camera. The last photo caught the two Americans' faces through the windshield. The messenger checked the quality of the shots on the view screen of his camera before leaving quietly.

Chapter 5
Seoul

Wook picked at the nasty scar on the surface of his desk with his fingernail. The small splintered wood had been making him increasingly angry and nervous. With his other hand, he held the phone tight to his ear and listened intently. "Everything is ready. We are planning on destroying the facility tomorrow. There will be nothing left of the building. The gas carrier will also be destroyed, but that means it cannot be traced."

"Are you certain that the vessel can be controlled?" asked Wook, who had serious doubts about the plan.

"Yes, sir. We tested it today. The system works. No problems at all, but we have to proceed at a slow speed to maintain control."

"Good," replied the aging director. "Do not call me when it is over. I will certainly see it on the news. Just make sure there are no complications." He hung up, pulled a silk handkerchief out of his breast pocket, and tried to polish the blemish on his desk. The fabric snagged on the splintered wood. The old man cursed his carelessness.

Chapter 6
Portsmouth

"Joe, you promised that you'd be home in a couple of days. Now, it's a week." Dalia played out the dramatics on Zoom just enough for Joe to realize that she was not really mad but instead just pulling his leg. Still, he truly didn't like being away from her for such a long time. The computer screen was not a substitute for caressing her dark hair or holding her face.

"By the way," commented Dalia, looking off the screen and down at her office desk, "I came up with some interesting hits on Hong Lines. It took a lot of work and digging, and I had to get some help from a friend who does research for one of the big banks. It looks like Hong significantly maxed out their loans with the banks about three years ago. Nearly a half-billion dollars to help with the new ships they were building, but some of their ships are now laid up with the weak economy and their sailing schedules have been slowed down."

"Probably slowing down their ships to save on expensive fuel," Joe remarked.

"Maybe, but how is Hong Lines paying off those loans while they are still taking delivery of a half-dozen new ships and covering all the overhead with the decrease in service?" she asked.

"Good question. And the shipping rates have been coming down for the last couple of years. Somehow they are getting their hands on money and I bet it is not by operating a steamship line. Have you tried going through their corporate reports?"

Dalia frowned before responding, "That's part of the problem, Joe. It's a family-owned company. They're not publicly traded. There are no corporate records I can look at. What little I have found out is from trade publications and the internet. We need some inside help."

"Let me think that over. Maybe Bob Connor at the State Department can help. He owes me for some work I did for them on the Law of the Sea convention. Why don't you give him a call and sweet talk him into helping us?"

"My sweet talking didn't get you back to New York any sooner, but I'll give it a try."

"Good. And Dalia, I promise that when I get back home, we will go see a show and have a fantastic dinner in Manhattan. You pick the restaurant. I'm pretty sure I'll fly back in two or three days. Ken and I just have to take a cruise in the harbor."

Dalia smiled and blew a kiss before leaning over to turn off her computer. "I'm not even going to ask what a cruise in the harbor is all about. Love you." The screen went blank.

Joe made some notes about what Dalia had said and then called Mike Graham in London to report on their new findings. Joe questioned whether the East of England could look into the location of the Master of the *Crazy Horse*. "I'm beginning to think that the Captain knows more than he is claiming," he commented to the club manager. Mike responded that he would have someone inquire.

About twenty minutes later, Joe and Ken met in the downstairs lobby of the funky Ship Leopard Hotel located just across the street from the beach in Portsmouth. The address said they were on the Hard, a street that took them directly to Boat House Number 4 with a leisurely walk. As they passed the familiar dock with the PT boat, Captain Ken mentioned that his grandfather had served on a torpedo patrol boat during WWII. They were powerful and fast, but predominantly made out of light plywood, which did little to bounce bullets.

This time it was a lot easier getting into the private research facility through the back door. Yeoman Fox was primping her short cut hair as they walked into the tank room. She glanced at Captain Ken, who, for the first time, acknowledged her flirting. He had gone through an unfortunate divorce several years earlier as a result of the fallout from the disastrous grounding of his vessel. As far as Joe was aware, Ken had not dated since the divorce. Instead, he spent a considerable amount of time with his two kids, who lived with their mother in a nearby town in New Jersey.

"What's on the menu for today, Ms. Fox?" asked Joe.

"The researchers intend to tow the sub out of the testing tank and into the cove. They want to see if the magnetic drive can be started. They are doing this outdoors in case of any potential fire or explosion. If they succeed, further repairs will be made to the nose of the vessel before it is actually allowed to navigate on its own for any distance.

Inside the building, they observed an eighteen-foot, semi-inflatable outboard boat that was positioned to the right of the sub and secured in place with several lines. Two navy personnel were testing the tautness of the lines. Dr. Locke stood on the pool platform, taking it all in. He finally gave a thumbs-up to an officer who was at the steering wheel of the zodiac. One of the research men popped his head out from the hatch and also signaled that all was good. The froth from behind the outboard prop began to build, with a wisp of white smoke, and slowly, the tandem crafts moved out from under the roof of the boat house.

Dr. Locke walked up to Joe and Ken and urged them to follow him down to the pier for a better view. He was obviously very excited and confident that they would be able to start the unique propulsion system.

Chapter 6

As they walked down the pier, Joe noticed that the tourists, who had lined up to board the *HMS Warrior*, were suddenly moving towards the far end of the dock to stare at something in the harbor. In the distance, the sounds of several loud and powerful ship horns could be heard blowing repeatedly. Both Joe and Ken stared in the same direction towards Gosport, which was a neck of land on the other side of the channel. A bright green, square-shaped vessel, shaped somewhat like a humpback whale, was slowly cutting across the crowded channel. It was forcing vessels in the traffic lanes to turn hard so as to avoid being struck by the floating blimp. Some of the tourists gasped as a small sailboat handled by two teenagers just missed being run over by the plodding ship, but what alarmed Joe the most was that the ship was turning in a jerky motion and appeared to be aiming itself right at the boathouse. While it was doing no more than five knots, it would be on top of them in less than twenty minutes.

Captain Ken looked through the telescopic lens on his camera. "That's an LNG self-propelled barge. See the two huge tanks on its deck? If that thing hits the pier, it will probably cause a massive explosion. Funny thing is that I don't see anyone on the bridge or the deck of the barge, but it is steering a deliberate course."

"I think it's aiming for the boathouse. Any ideas?" Joe asked. Captain Ken carefully took in everything around them, and perked up.

"Yeah, but it's a long shot. Follow me. Yeoman Fox, I suggest you call your Coast Guard and alert them to what is happening. Meanwhile, Dr. Locke, tell the zodiac to bring the mini-sub back into the shed then tell everyone to get off this pier and out of the Boat House. If that barge explodes, there won't be much left of this area of the town. It will be worse than the Texas City disaster, which maimed over thirty-five-hundred people and left a firestorm after it blew up." "My God," said Dr. Locke as he dashed off towards the security guards at the base of the boarding ladder to the historic battleship. Joe followed Captain Ken's long strides down the pier. When they reached the PT Boat that was tied up to the dock, Ken hopped over the railing and onto its forward deck. The boat appeared empty. "Joe, start to loosen the lines, both front and back. I've got to go below and start the engines." Joe immediately began to pull off the lines from the bollards on the pier and tossed them onto the patrol boat.

Captain Ken slid down the ladder into the engine room. Three massive engines, each capable of producing about 1200 horsepower, gleamed even with the poor lighting. An old man in a dirty boiler suit, with his back towards Ken, was tinkering at the work desk. He turned when Ken hit the floorboards. He was obviously surprised. His white beard, blue eyes, and weathered face fit in perfectly with the old PT boat. "What are you doing here, son?" he asked in an obvious American accent. "No one is allowed on board."

"Yes, sir," remarked Ken, "but we have a real emergency coming down on us. There is an LNG barge in the harbor that seems to be out of control and heading our way. This whole place is going to blow in less than twenty minutes. I've got to get this boat moving and see if we can knock that barge off course."

"Why didn't you say so?", the old man grinned with huge white teeth. "Been waiting over fifty years for something to happen to get 'Old Belle' back into service. You turn off the magnetos over on the wall and let me open the coolant."

"OK. Magnetos are off."

"Good, now go to that board on the starboard wall and turn on the battery banks. Once you get that done, I'll get the ignition power on and start the compressor. Fuel line is already on as I was working on a gauge." Two minutes later, with a permanent smile now painted on his face, the old man yelled "Clear!" and pressed the solenoid button for the port engine. There was a pause and a cough, followed by the sound of the massive engine turning over, slowly at first, and then gaining speed. "She's got oil pressure!" said the old man, who looked at the board and adjusted his wire-frame glasses. He continued to hold the large back starter button. Fifteen seconds later, the starboard engine was coughing and belching, but she was obviously running. Within seconds, both engines began to purr.

The old man pointed at the third starter button. "Probably won't be able to start the middle engine. She's been finicky. But the two outboard units will give this boat plenty of power." Ken could hear the flush of cooling water being discharged over both sides and gave the thumbs up to the bearded engineer. He then ran up the ladder and sprinted to the steering wheel. Straight ahead, maybe a little over a thousand yards, was the green barge with the white tanks. Boats all over the harbor were at a standstill, facing the barge and sounding their horns. Ken could also see emergency workers on the pier pointing the visitors to run to shore. People were fleeing the pier, some stumbling along the way.

"Joe," yelled Ken over the din of the loud engines, "there's an old guy in the engine room; a mechanic or something. Yell down the hatch and tell him to give me forward speed."

Stunned that someone occupied the engine room, Joe leaned over the hatch opening. He could not see anyone, but trusted Ken nonetheless. "Captain Ken says we need forward speed right now. Can you hear me?" A moment later, there was a distorted reply between the rumbles of the engines.

"OK… I'll... start with the… port side first."

A heavy clunk could be heard below deck. Vessel engines belched black smoke out the side vents. Slowly, the PT boat picked up speed and then there was a second "clunk" as the starboard engine was brought online. A white froth could be seen slipping out behind the stern wake.

A moment later, the white-bearded man came out of the hatch, climbing the steps with the agility of a man half his age. He moved forward to the helm, where Ken had the wheel and Joe was focusing the camera's telescopic lens on the barge. Joe finally commented, "I'm telling you that there is no one on that barge; either that or they are all dead."

"She's steering kind of erratic, as if there was a kid at the wheel, huh," said the old man.

Ken looked over at the mechanic's face and smiled. "Sure glad you were down there. Not sure I could have started her. My name is Ken, by the way, and this is my boss, Joe. We're from New York."

"Names Marc Newcomb, originally from Norfolk, Virginia." "How did you get on a PT boat in Portsmouth, England?" asked Joe.

"Volunteer. I spent my last years in the U.S. Navy preserving some of the old PT boats."

They watched the looming barge whose course was unchanged. It was headed straight towards the Boat House. "That's a really big barge. You weren't planning on shooting it with that machine gun, were you?" Joe pointed at the 50-caliber machine gun mounted on the front deck of the PT boat.

"That gun ain't fired in years, and besides, there are no bullets on board," said Newcomb. "Torpedo tubes are empty too. Got some ball bearings down below you can throw at the barge if you want."

Ken chuckled, which did not comfort his boss. "No, Joe. You wouldn't want to shoot that barge filled with liquid natural gas, especially with tracer bullets. It would create the largest fireworks display in your lifetime which, by the way, would be the last fireworks you would briefly see. Nope, my plan is to nudge the bow of our boat up against the barge and push like hell in the hope that we can divert the vessel over towards the mud bank, which you can see about 100 yards beyond the boathouse. With a little bit of luck, the barge goes aground and is stuck in the mud and we all get to live."

CHAPTER 6

"You know, Dalia will kill you if I die," Joe retorted with a smile on his face.

"Yes, I figured that. However, before she does that, she first has to piece me back together." Ken increased speed and spray started coming over the bow in spritzes. White foam was now all around the PT boat as it began to plane. "Alright, Joe, get all the rubber fenders on this boat and tie them on the rail up at the bow. Set them high up, on the left side. They have to fill the space between the rail of our boat and the side of the barge. Mr. Newcomb, you may need to get that third engine started if all else fails. You think there is any chance you can do that?"

"Yes, sir. I'll get her started. Just don't know what kind of power we can get out of her. You are going to have to baby all the engines. They were never designed to be used like a tugboat, and now they are nearly eighty years old." The old mechanic deftly disappeared into the engine compartment.

As Joe walked cautiously towards the front of the speeding patrol boat, he looked up at the bridge of the LNG barge. It was clear that no one was on the bridge. "How the hell is she steering herself?" thought Joe. He then grabbed a half-dozen tube-shaped fenders made of heavy rubber and tied them tightly along the outer-most edge of the boat near the bow. He had tremendous confidence in Captain Ken, but he had some real doubts about this plan. The barge, while not as large as an ocean-going ship, still towered over them. The main deck of the LNG carrier was at least another eight feet higher than the PT boat. The ship was perhaps even more imposing because of its somewhat square shape and its stubby front end. The two massive cylinder tanks on deck were at least twenty feet high and twice as long. They cast a shadow on the water as the sun behind the ship was blocked out of view. Ken skillfully brought the PT boat around in a U-turn parallel to the barge and closed the distance to the green hull. He pulled back on the throttle to maintain the same speed as the barge. Slowly, he pulled alongside near the bow of the barge. For the first time, both Ken and Joe noticed an old rope ladder hanging over the side of the barge. Capt. Ken firmly but carefully turned the wheel over so that the PT boat did a controlled collision with the giant barge just forward of the ladder. The inflated fenders squealed and hissed in protest as they became squashed between the two hulls. Slowly, Captain Ken increased the power on both engines and more black smoke began to belch from the exhaust ports on both sides of the boat. The huge motors could be heard growling and rumbling below deck. Ken continued to keep the wheel hard over so as to push the barge to the left of its intended course and towards the mud bank. However, as soon as the barge seemed to slightly alter direction, Ken could feel it push back towards its original course. It looked like they had undertaken a useless exercise.

Ken then yelled out to Joe, "Climb the ladder. Get on board the barge and see if you can shut down the bridge. I think it is still under some sort of control. Use your cell phone to contact me."

Joe's fear of heights was forgotten in the overwhelming danger of the situation. He climbed up the unwieldy and crude rope rungs, threw himself over the railing to the barge's deck, and sprinted towards the bridge house. There was an outside emergency stairwell built into the steel bulkhead that lead to the raised deck where the bridge was located. Joe bounded up the steps two at a time as he watched Boat House No. 4 getting closer. The end of the pier was now less than five hundred yards away. Once on the bridge level, Joe tore the door open and stepped inside. It was empty and eerily quiet. The small steering wheel mounted on a pedestal in the center of the room was unmanned, but he could see it turn in sporadic spurts. At that moment, Joe also noted a laptop computer sitting open just in front of the wheel on the window ledge, but its screen was oddly facing out the huge glass window. Joe carefully picked up the laptop, noting that a long thick cable ran to a USB port on the control panel at the captain's station. When he looked at the screen, he realized he was looking at a close up image of himself that moved when he moved. The camera in the screen was obviously on! Joe immediately closed the screen shut and jerked out the USB cable. He then put the computer down on the navigation table to call Ken on the mobile phone. Just as Ken answered, the laptop began to smoke. Small, yellow sparks flew out of the casing. The smell of burning plastic was overwhelming. A small flame erupted from the bottom of the unit.

Joe yelled into the phone, "Wait a second," as he pushed the laptop away with a set of metal dividers from the paper charts and manuals on the navigation station.

"Ken, there was a laptop on the bridge that had its camera pointing out the forward window. It was linked to the command station by cable. I think someone hacked into the ship's computer and was steering the barge."

"Joe, you must have done something right because I am now making some progress pushing the front of the barge. Turn the ship's wheel. See if that works."

Joe immediately took the little wheel, which looked like it came off a riding lawn mower, and tried to turn it hard over to the left. It barely moved. "Ken, she won't budge. The wheel must be locked. And I can't find any emergency shut off for the engines. It must be down in the engine room. Any other suggestions?"

"Yeah, get the hell out of there. You may need to jump into the water if we are going up on those rocks."

The PT boat and the barge were now less than three hundred yards from the Boat House. Joe raced down the stairwell. He could still see the flashing blue lights of a few police cars lined up along the shoreline. Police were frantically waving people to move back. Ken called back to Newcomb, whose head had appeared above the hatch like a gopher. "Mr. Newcomb, we really need that third engine on line. We are running out of water." Newcomb ducked down and ran to the panel on the sidewall. "Pray the old lady will start." He pushed the black rubber button with his palm.

There was a startling backfire, then a second. After a moment of silence, the engine caught and began to turn over roughly. The middle engine was vibrating and twisting on her blocks. "Great job, Mr. Newcomb," Ken yelled over the din. "Now, give me maximum power!"

Black, oily smoke drifted everywhere, engulfing the PT boat in a dirty fog. Joe climbed down the rope ladder trying to cover his nose with the sleeve of his jacket. As he touched down on the top deck, he could feel the entire length of the PT boat twerking and shuddering as it tried to push against the massive barge.

The course of the barge was steadily, but very slowly, shifting away from the Boat House. That was the good news. However, Joe could see that barge was still headed for the edge of the rocky shoals along the beach line. The barge had not shifted enough to go into the mud bank. Ken was standing at the wheel, gritting his teeth, and pulling on the steering wheel with all his strength.

Several helicopters were now overhead, including one belonging to the Royal Coast Guard. Two other choppers appeared to be with local news stations as cameras were held out the aircraft doors to photograph the scene. Suddenly, Newcomb was again at their sides. "Sorry Captain. That's all the power I can get out of the three ladies. And I expect the engines are going to start failing one by one in a couple of minutes. They haven't been subjected to this kind of overload since the war."

Ken kept his eyes on the bow and noticed that the swing of the barge's nose was gaining speed. Within moments, it was clear that they were now definitely aimed at the mud bank. Joe looked at Ken with a quizzical expression on his face. Ken simply shrugged. They both heard the repeated horn of an unseen boat on the other side of the barge. At the same time, Joe's cell phone began to vibrate in his pocket. Joe picked it up, not recognizing the number on the screen. "Hello?" he said.

"Yes, right. Sure you were not expecting this call, but Dr. Locke gave us your number. We are on a pilot boat in the harbor and got an emergency message to help you fellows out. We are now pushing on the opposite side of the barge, back at the stern. Don't think you can see us. But the extra push seems to have done the trick. Gather you fellows are trying to redirect our runaway barge into the mud flats in front of us. Brilliant idea."

"Thank God. Wasn't sure we would make it there for a moment," said Joe over the phone. He then turned to Ken and Newcomb and yelled over the deafening noise, "A pilot boat is pushing the stern of the barge on the other side. That's why she is turning faster. What do you want me to tell them?"

Ken studied the situation in front of him. "We are going to have to pull away in a few minutes; otherwise, we are going to get caught in the mud bank as well. I am a bit worried the barge may run over us if we remain in this position. Tell them to keep pushing until we are out of here."

Joe relayed the information to the pilot boat, whose Captain agreed that the PT boat had to get out of the path of the barge immediately.

"Understood. And once again, thanks for the help." Joe hung up and stuffed the phone back in his pocket. "Let's get out of here, Ken." At that very moment, a large bang could be heard from below deck, followed by a huge puff of heavy grey smoke that billowed out of the engine-room hatch.

Newcomb looked up from the hatch and then said to Ken firmly, "Just lost engine number 3. Better pull back on the throttle for the other engines. I think you have done all that is possible."

Gradually, the throttle was pulled back and Ken reluctantly turned the wheel all the way over, and steered away from the huge barge. The old PT boat glided away from the side of the ship. Moments later, the LNG tanker seemed to shudder before slowly digging herself into the mud bank. Her squared-off bow seemed to dip down, while the stern of the vessel rose slightly in the air. The giant barge jerked as her speed came to a halt, water still thrashing out from her stern. The Coast Guard helicopter lowered itself to a few feet off the forward deck of the stuck barge. Two ropes were thrown out each side of the aircraft. Within seconds, half a dozen men were down the ropes and headed towards the bridge. Most were carrying assault rifles. Joe continued to scan the upper levels of the barge, but there was still no sign of any humans.

Ken steered the PT boat back to the pier and neatly pulled alongside the pilings. Some black and blue smoke still puffed out of the exhaust, but two of the engines continued to run. After the lines were tied to the cleats, Captain Ken instructed Newcomb to shut down the engines. There was a rumble, some pops, and a cough, and then the giant motors went dead. Afterward, there was only the sound of the coolant water still being pumped overboard. Newcomb's soot-covered head came up through the hatch and he was wiping his forehead with a red-checkered bandanna. The grin on his face was ear-to-ear. "Both engines are overheated. I'll probably need a month to get them back in top working condition, but it was worth it just to see Old Belle prove she still had it in her. But I am not so sure the Brits are going to appreciate what you did to their PT boat."

Moments after the old mechanic's utterance, Commander Heard, Yeoman Fox, and Dr. Locke could be seen walking briskly on the pier in their direction. They did not seem particularly happy, and each carried a very official face. Meanwhile, helicopters continued to swirl overhead and crowds were gathering along the seawall to look at the huge gas barge now stuck in the mud. Some were applauding. The commander was the first to step onto the deck of the PT boat while Capt. Ken checked the lines and secured the cockpit. Joe figured it was best to say they were sorry about the damage to the WWII boat before the criticism started. "Real sorry about any damage to the PT boat motors. Mr. Newcomb here assures us it can be repaired."

"Gentlemen, damn the engines. Do you realize what you have just done? You probably saved the lives of several thousand people, including our navy personnel living on the base. Not only do we still have the submersible, the Boat House, and the Naval base all intact, but the *HMS Warrior* as well. That was a brilliant piece of navigation, Captain Ken, and we are all in your debt. God knows how that barge got out of control."

Joe looked at the barge sitting near the shoreline and then said to the naval officer, "I think your men will find a burned-out laptop on the barge's bridge. I suspect someone climbed on board while she was at anchor using the Jacob's ladder we found hanging over the bow. Then, they set up the laptop so it was facing out the window and plugged it into the Captain's station. They were using the camera on the computer to steer the barge. They hacked into the ship's own computer and taken control over most systems. I pulled the cable out of the computer, but seconds later, the computer went up in smoke. I suspect it was destroyed remotely."

The look on Commander Heard's face was one of grave concern. "Our Coast Guard just signaled me that they discovered a burned-out laptop after boarding the barge. They are sending it to a lab to see if there is enough of it left to determine who was hacking the ship. Once again, gentlemen, Her Majesty's government thanks you."

Ken reached out and shook the hand of the commander and simply said, "We were in the right place at the wrong time. The real thanks go to Mr. Newcomb here who has kept this beautiful piece of American naval art alive and working."

Newcomb rubbed his beard, taking the compliment in stride. "Many people don't know it, but the United States sent a lot of Higgens-built PT boats to England and Russia at the beginning of World War II," Newcomb said. "They were equipped with Packard engines, just like this one. When I heard this boat was undergoing restoration about ten years ago, I volunteered. I was retired, sitting home doing nothing and my dear wife had passed away. So, I came over and told the Royal Navy I was willing to assist in the maintenance of the boat. They were happy to have me, and I haven't gone home since."

"If those engines hadn't started, the situation would have been no different than if we had jumped into a rowboat," Ken said.

Commander Heard turned to the bearded mechanic. "It was a good show. We owe you our deep gratitude, Mr. Newcomb." I will make sure you get all the funds and parts needed to make any repairs. This patrol boat has done a miraculous job."

Newcomb smiled and responded, "Promise I will have her running like new. Glad I could help."

Commander Heard then instructed the yeoman to arrange for Joe and Ken to be flown back to London by helicopter. The Navy would take care of the return on their rental car. "Frankly, Mr. Barrett, I am doing this to keep you out of the press. They will be hounding you at the first opportunity. You are to say nothing about the laptop onboard the barge, the sub, or what goes on in Boat House 4. I think you understand." The naval officer smartly stepped off the PT boat and walked with his junior officer towards the battleship.

Joe and Ken grabbed their gear from the car in the parking lot and met the yeoman in an open field at the end of the street. Not more than five minutes later, the heavy thump of a large copter could be heard approaching their position. A Westland Sea King flew in low from the north and circled before settling down gently on the grass. The door immediately opened and an airman signaled to the yeoman to get the two men on board and keep their heads low. As Joe picked up his bag and leaned into the wind blast from the slow rotating blades, he could see Ken talking to Yeoman Fox before picking up his own bag. She whispered something into the captain's ear before he turned and started walking towards the helicopter. Joe was fairly certain Ken was grinning.

The huge aircraft landed at the Barclay's London heliport, more commonly known as Battersea. A black Range Rover and driver were waiting for Barrett and the captain as they exited the field office. In less than an hour, they were climbing out of the car at the entrance to their hotel.

Joe kept looking over his shoulder for the hordes of paparazzi that he was anticipating based on Commander Heard's warning. So far, there were none. However, when he picked up his key at the concierge desk at the hotel, a story covering the incident in Portsmouth came on the overhead television in the lobby. Joe stared in disbelief as he watched a clip filmed by one of the helicopters. The video clearly showed Joe and Ken on the PT boat as it tried desperately to push the huge LNG tanker barge out of its path towards the Boat House. At one point, Newcomb could be seen poking his head out of the access to the engine room and talking to them. Words on a red banner scrolling beneath the video read: "UNIDENTIFIED MEN SAVE PORTSMOUTH FROM POTENTIAL DISASTER." Joe turned to Ken who was watching the same screen. The young lady in the neat suit and white blouse, with the name-plate "Poppy," returned to the desk and handed Joe his plastic key card together with a couple of messages. Noting all the attention to the television, she looked up at the screen and then looked at the two men in front of her. The look on her face made it clear she had made the connection. Joe immediately turned and grabbed Ken by the elbow. “We have got to check out now. The concierge just figured out who we are.”

Fifteen minutes later, the two men were at the check-out desk. The young lady at the concierge desk was pointing them out to some of her colleagues and whispering excitedly. There was at least one desk clerk, an older gentleman, who had a dubious look on his face. He kept checking his watch. Joe figured he was probably trying to understand how they could be in London when the news was reporting that the barge grounded only an hour before. Joe decided to forgo the underground to Heathrow and jumped into a waiting black cab with Ken. Minutes later, they were on the Embankment headed towards the airport. Joe picked up his cell phone and dialed.

“Well, I can see that you and Ken enjoyed your cruise in the harbor,” were Dalia’s words upon answering the phone.

Joe slowly responded, “Let me guess. You saw us on TV?”

“Yup, and so has the whole office. You’re famous now, which is why I won’t kill you when you get back home. That was a pretty crazy stunt you two pulled. And I saw you climb the rope ladder.”

“I may have cured my fear of heights,” responded Joe, knowing that was probably not the best answer.

“You’re alive. That’s all I care about. Where are you now?”

“On our way to the airport. We are trying to get out of here before the reporters catch up”.

“Well, Mr. McDonald left me a note saying that he would like to see you first thing upon your arrival back in the office.” McDonald was the crusty old managing partner of the firm who did not always see eye to eye with Barrett. “I don’t think from his expression that he is going to give you a medal.”

“Got it. Anything more on Hong Lines?”

"No," Dalia said with some exasperation. "The more I dig, the more rock I run into. Something fishy is going on, but I think I may have found a new source of information with help from Julie Mai, the paralegal in corporate. She speaks Mandarin."

Joe looked at Ken and then followed up with one more question. "Any luck on finding companies that could have made the Pilot Fish?"

"Yeah. I was about to send an email to you. There is a company in Genoa, Italy, that seems to have recently made some news in the trade journals about advanced developments in compact magnetic drives. It is not clear if they are building submarines, but they do have connections with local shipbuilders. Anyway, Joe, it is the best lead yet."

"How's your Italian?"

"Molto bene, signore. You know my dad was born in Italy."

Joe smiled, and replied, "Well, maybe it's time you join me on a little vacation to Liguria; should be nice this time of year."

There was a long pause on the phone. Finally, Dalia giggled and responded, "Do I need to bring a gun?"

Chapter 7
Gangnam

Wook was quiet but furious inside. He was trimming the branches on a small tree in the tidy little garden outside of his home. He could hear his phone ringing in the study, just a few feet away. The door was open, but he had no intention of answering the call. The news broadcast on the television was a disaster. Some half-century-old patrol boat had managed to push the LNG-filled barge out of its intended course. He had anticipated watching a video on the news about the results of a major explosion and fire in Portsmouth, which would have destroyed the boat house and the submersible, but instead, every channel was carrying photographs of three men who had diverted his barge with a World War II-era oversized yacht. *Ridiculous*, he thought.

When he first saw the news, he immediately called Jian, who had put together the technical operation for the barge. He had a lot of confidence in Jian; they had gone to school together as children. The old engineer apologized profusely to Wook, expecting that he was out of a job. He reminded the director that he had warned that remote steerage of the barge required the vessel to move at very slow speeds to accommodate the software override. "The real problem, Mr. Director, is that someone climbed up on the barge just before it was about to strike the building. That person disengaged the computer from the bridge. I was compensating for the pushing from the old boat, but once we lost remote control, there was nothing we could do."

"Do we know if he was the Royal Navy or Coast Guard?" asked Hong Wook.

"No, sir. It was a man I have not seen before. He looked directly into our computer camera. His picture was taken. I have sent it to you," Jin replied.

The old man clicked on a couple of the keys to his computer and stared at Joe's face, cocked to one side, with squinted eyes and a quizzical expression. "I don't understand. Who is this man?"

"We have access to our government's facial recognition program. My staff is trying to make a match. So far, we have had no luck. Again, my apologies, Director."

Wook slammed the phone down and walked into the still night air and his well-groomed garden in hopes of calming himself. Who was this man who defeated his elaborate plan?

"I think I can help you identify the person who interfered with the explosion of the barge," said a familiar voice from a dark corner in the yard bordered by a bamboo wall. Wook felt himself shiver. It was the damn messenger. Wook turned and walked back towards the study in the hope of forcing the messenger to walk into the light. He did not need this visit.

"He is an American; so is his friend. Look on your desk." Wook Hong saw the photograph laying in front of him. It was a bit grainy, and there was some reflection off the windshield, but the same face as the man on the bridge of the gas carrier was staring out the window of a car. At the driver's seat was a slightly older man, blond hair with a beard. He was the man who was driving the PT boat during the television clip.

"Who are they?" was all that the director said.

"Joe Barrett and Ken Libby. They work for an American law firm. They handle maritime cases. My information indicates they were hired by a London insurance company to investigate the collision of the *Crazy Horse.*"

"Do they know about the submersible?"

"Yes," said the messenger as he placed a thin folder on the director's desk. "In fact, they have been inside the sub. The insurance company probably wants to know where the sub came from."

The director chuckled. "So does everyone else. Why should I worry about some American lawyers? Are they going to sue me?"

The messenger remained in the shadow. He responded quietly, "You may be right. There is nothing to worry about, but they have been very resourceful so far. I understand their law firm has been checking up on you and your company."

Wook felt a pang in his stomach and sat down. The situation was continuing to get worse. "They won't find anything," the old man finally said in a quiet voice.

"Good, because my employer would be very unhappy if they determine the real purpose of the submarine."

"Well, then, why don't you get rid of them? Certainly, that is something you are good at, am I correct?" hearing no response, the director turned in his chair and looked at the open door.

"Am I correct?" he said more forcefully, but the messenger had already left.

Chapter 8
Jongno

Captain Bo-Hee Park hadn't been able to get a good night's sleep since the collision of his vessel, the *Crazy Horse*, with the *Viking Trader*. He knew something was not right. He did not believe that his employer, Hong Lines, was telling him the full truth. He had been assigned to the ship since it came out of the construction yard in Pusan. The vessel had performed almost flawlessly until about two weeks ago, when there were reports of strange noises from the bottom of the ship that could not be traced. The helmsman had complained about the vessel drifting off course. Then, there was the failure of the auxiliary electrical plant, followed by the collision. It was only then that the God-forsaken leech was found stuck to the bottom of his ship. How long had it been there? The small submarine probably accounted for the steering and the electrical problems.

After being pulled into port, his ship had been immediately arrested by the owners of the cargo onboard. The captain was certain he would be jailed as well, but apparently, British courts were not like those in the Far East, which often charge the Master with the crimes of the vessel. Still, the company had not visited him, nor given him any indication of whether he would be reassigned to a new ship. He had expected at least a note from the director, whom he had known for nearly two decades, but there had been no contact.

While he had fully cooperated with the British authorities and the Royal Navy, he had left out one piece of information.

The day after the vessel left the port of Colon, on the Caribbean side of the Panama Canal, Mr. Hong called him via satellite phone. What appeared to be pleasantries and an attempt to find out how the new ship was performing ended with a strange instruction by the director to have the vessel idle off the coast of Panama for precisely two hours at a specific coordinate. Wook Hong explained his request by suggesting that there might be a need to go back into Colon for some additional cargo. However, the captain was told that if he received no further directions in that time period, then the ship was to proceed onto Antwerp. No entry was to be taken in the ship's log about the delay. The two hours passed and Captain Park gave orders to continue their voyage across the Atlantic. In his thirty years at sea, he had never received such a strange order. It was after that event that all the strange happenings began. The captain was certain that the submarine had attached itself during those two hours of waiting. But why? He had no answer.

The old mariner got out of his bed and grunted as he walked to the small kitchen. The arthritis in his knees was taking its toll again. As he passed through the small living room, Park saw the curtain blowing from the gentle breeze outside. He scratched the bottom of his eye, wondering why he had left the door open. He gave the cedar door a soft tug and it slid smoothly and silently into its track.

The tea kettle brought the water to a boil in a few minutes. The Captain took some of his favorite traditional tea out of the canister. It was a special blend of roots, flowers, sweet fruits, mushrooms, and some seaweed. He allowed the tea to steep for several minutes before taking a sip. The aroma was wonderful, even if the taste was a bit bitter. Captain Park returned to his bed and placed the cup down on the side table after several more sips. He was a little light-headed but was amazed at how drowsy he felt. The captain lay his head on the pillow, pulled up the cover, and waited for sleep.

Chapter 8

Captain Park, a well-respected and knowledgeable Master of vessels of all tonnage and all seas, never awoke. It was said that he died in his sleep. However, one of the investigators from Pusan found it curious that there was no tea, nor any teacups in the house when his body was found a day later. *Didn't everyone like traditional tea*, the inspector thought.

Chapter 9
New York

"Mr. Barrett, I hope you know what you are doing! You are on the verge of getting this venerable firm into the news media, and for more than one hundred years, we have successfully avoided the unwarranted light of the media." Old man McDonald, in his starched, custom-made Egyptian shirt and Italian handmade silk tie, poked nervously at the folder on his desk. It was apparently filled with news clippings of the incident in Portsmouth, many with grainy photos of Joe and Ken on the PT boat. The Director of the firm was genuinely upset, which Barrett thought a bit odd given the firm's efforts to compete with the other Legal 500 law firms in the midtown Manhattan neighborhood. How could saving a town in the United Kingdom from explosion and disaster possibly be unwarranted media attention? Other firms would be trying to capitalize on the heroic efforts by their employees, which Joe suddenly realized was not what he personally wanted at the moment, given the sensitive nature of his investigation.

"Sir, I assure you that we had no intention of placing the firm in harm's way. We have avoided interviews with the press, and we have no intention of giving statements to the newspapers. Indeed, even the client wants us to keep this hush-hush."

Mr. McDonald looked up, his face a bit weary. After a pause, he then said, "I must say that I am still not certain what you boys have gotten yourselves into. All I've heard is it has something to do with submarines. Why do you have to go all the way to England to look at submarines? Drive up to Groton, Connecticut. They're all over the place."

"Yes, sir. That's a good idea." Joe stood up, and as he was about to leave, he realized the meeting in McDonald's office provided a rare opportunity to speak about another matter. "Sir, if I might just discuss one other matter, unrelated to the submarine?"

"Yes, go ahead. I have a few minutes before the executive committee meeting."

"Well, sir," Joe coughed, not sure he really wanted to complete the sentence, "you may be aware that my paralegal, Dalia and I have been seeing each other?"

"It has come to my attention. I appreciate your bringing up the subject. In fact, I have been meaning to talk to you about that."

Joe gulped, realizing he may have accelerated the drop of the guillotine.

McDonald stood up straight and walked over to Joe. He looked Barrett squarely in the eye, and then put his hand out. "I wish the two of you the best of luck. She has done marvels at molding your behavior. Frankly, I had given up on you as a young maverick. But since Dalia has come into the firm you are indeed demonstrating to be a new man. You have my blessing, Joe."

Joe shook the old man's hand two or three times, not believing what he had heard. He was about to respond and ask if there wasn't an issue with firm policy. McDonald caught his eye, and Joe instantly understood that he was not to go there.

"Just make sure you invite me to the wedding, Joe. And if you don't marry her, well, you're a damn fool." He grabbed a file off his desk and headed out the door.

Joe returned to his office with a relieved expression on his face. He deliberately passed by Dalia's desk, which was situated in a carol in the hallway. Dalia was working on a spreadsheet, her face inches from the screen checking the numbers. Joe leaned over and kissed her head from behind. She was so focused on the screen that she just swatted the back of her head.

"I have some good news, and some even better news," said Barrett, realizing that Dalia was still not aware of his presence.

The beautiful head of black hair swirled in eddies as she swiveled around in her chair. Dalia's face lit up with a smile, realizing whose voice it was. Jewel-green eyes looked up at Joe.

"Joe. It's you. I think I discovered something important."

"You didn't hear a word I said. OK. You go first."

"The records that we got on the internet yesterday indicate that Hong Lines owns a company in Shanghai called KS Dailren, which handles many of the ship agency functions in China."

"OK," said Joe, "what's so unusual about that? Lots of steamship lines have their own agencies in foreign countries to help with arrangements when their ships come into port."

"I know. But KS Dailren apparently owns or has some legal interest in several other companies organized in China. One of them, Bei Mei, if I pronounced it right, is involved with North Korea. The company has received huge contracts with the Chinese government for the supply of coal from North Korea.

"Which would put them in direct conflict with U.S. sanctions involving North Korea," reflected Barrett. "Whose ships are they using to transport the coal?"

"Well, that's why you pay me the huge bucks around here. I'm not positive, but I think Hong Lines is using their own ships, the ones that supposedly have been laid up. Hard to be certain, but there seems to be a discrepancy in the count of Hong's ships that are not under charter."

"Where are the non-working vessels laid up?"

"In the port of Yantai," she replied.

Joe's face glowed. "Which is just across the straight from North Korea! That's brilliant. I don't know yet how it all ties in, but I am certain that Hong Lines must have a connection with the government of North Korea, which is somehow behind the submarine. "

Dalia brought up another page on her screen, a news article from Reuters. "You know that China ordered all its ships destined for North Korea to return the coal on board after repeated missile tests drew international criticism. However, Hong's vessels are registered in Liberia and are not subject to Chinese control. Hence, those ships may be providing the only way for coal to get out of North Korea at this time."

Dalia then swiveled to look back at the screen and asked, "so what is it that you have that is good and better news, huh?"

"You were listening, then. Well, the first good news is that I am taking you to dinner tonight."

"All right. I can get my mom to watch Daniel." Her son was eight and she had been raising him alone since her husband ran off less than a year after his birth. "And the better news? I am uncertain whether we are going to dinner just because you are tired of my cooking."

"I love your cooking! Honest, and I probably should wait till we dine tonight, but I just came from Mr. McDonald's office and he has given us his blessing. No more sneaking out for lunch."

Dalia's face was frozen, almost in a look of shock. Both had expected the firm to ask one of them to leave, and that probably meant Dalia as the last one in. Other romances in the office usually wound up with one partner having to leave.

"Joe, I don't know what to say. That's wonderful. No more hiding the truth, although everyone seems to know anyhow."

She grabbed him around the waist and drew him down for a full kiss on the lips. Joe started to resist but gave in.

From behind Barrett came a cough, and then deep voice, "Joe, if you can come up for air, there is a call coming in from Mike Graham." Capt. Ken winked at Dalia, and then he walked into Joe's office. He pressed the speaker phone button on Joe's phone and remarked that Barrett was engaged in the hallway and would be walking in momentarily. Joe flushed, pecked Dalia on the cheek, and walked into his office. He started talking before he reached his chair.

"Mike, hope all is well with you. Didn't realize you were going to call today."

"Joe, we have a problem."

Ken closed the door to the office, assuming it was going to be confidential information. "You know how you asked us to follow up on the location of the captain of the *Crazy Horse* so that you could interview him about the… the Pilot Fish?" Graham caught himself before mentioning the submarine.

"Sure. I'm ready to go interview him. He's the next key step."

"Yes. Well, afraid you won't be seeing him. He died two days ago. At home, in his sleep."

"Funny, I didn't think he was that old."

"He wasn't. Just turned fifty. Suspicious if you ask me. But the police have ruled it death by 'natural' causes.'"

Is the coroner going to do an autopsy?" asked Joe.

"Can't. Some distant family member immediately demanded custody of the body. He was cremated less than twenty-four hours later."

"This was all in Korea?"

"Yes. Pusan."

"Which is where Hong Lines has their offices?"

"What a coincidence, huh!" Mike said, with more than a hint of sarcasm in his voice.

Joe shuffled some papers on his desk, gaining time to think. He had not anticipated this development. "Mike, much as I know that the arrows are pointing to Hong Lines in Korea, I first need to go to Italy. I think we may have found someone who may know about the construction of the Pilot Fish, or at least its engines."

"Finally, some good news. Let me know what happens. And by the way, don't let me find any time on your firm's bills for performing superhero stunts in England. I don't pay you to play Tom Cruise."

Chapter 10
Genoa

The flight to Milan was less than eight hours, but Barrett's back was killing him when they landed at Malpensa Airport.

He rented a Fiat 500X, and in less than an hour, he and Dalia were headed south towards Genoa. The little car, with the 1.4-liter engine, had a lot more zip than Joe expected. Its all-wheel-drive performed well, the handling was agile, and frankly, Joe got a kick out of the manual transmission. He hadn't driven a stick-shift in years.

The road signs showed that they reached the town of Alessandria. Located in the Piedmont region of Italy, it was mostly vineyards and farms, but Joe loved the fact that it had a museum dedicated to Borsalino hats, the type his grandfather wore back in the fifties. The couple had lunch at Ristorazione Sociale, a small and inexpensive eatery with red walls and a wooden ceiling, before getting back on the highway to Genoa. The road twisted through the mountain gorges, which seemed to have little impact on the speed of the autos. Joe concentrated on the narrow lanes, and about an hour later, they could see the bright blue Mediterranean Sea off to the right. Soon, the road was running through increasingly long tunnels along the edge of the ocean, many constructed during the time of Mussolini. Finally, they entered onto an elevated roadway that curved around the waterside of Genoa. Joe exited the highway at the city center. A couple of turns and Joe was on Via Vente Setembre, a fashionable avenue in the heart of the city that had its sidewalks covered by galleries. Joe stopped in front of the Hotel Bristol, a stately old building near Piazza Ferrari that was probably two centuries old. Dalia took the luggage inside and Joe handed the car keys to the porter. The fireplace was burning in the waiting room just off the reception area, taking some of the chill off the early autumn air. After checking in, with the help of Dalia's grasp of Italian, the lift took them to the fifth floor, where their corner room was located.

"My God, Joe, look at the height of the ceiling in this room. It must be twenty-five feet." Dalia was mesmerized by the huge room, the chandelier, the polished parquet floors, the large armoire, and the closed-in terrace that overlooked the boulevard below them. Joe smiled. It was definitely not a Holiday Inn.

An hour later, Joe insisted they had to get out of the huge feather bed and dress. They walked several blocks, passing the house near the city wall that is believed to have belonged to Christopher Columbus. Finally, on Via Roma, Joe turned and climbed down a few steps to the doors of a local restaurant. The interior walls were made of stone with wood beam ceilings overhead. Only a few customers were eating, so there were plenty of empty tables. However, Joe immediately walked to a tall, thin, middle-aged man with long hair and wire-rim glasses sitting at a corner table. He had the look of a professor in his three-piece suit.

"Stefano, *come stai*?" said Joe with his open arms. The man turned and immediately smiled. His face reminded Dalia of Gene Wilder. "Joe, or maybe I should call you Giuseppe? You haven't aged a day. Come, sit with me. And be sure to place this lovely lady at my side." His Italian accent suggested that he could break into song at any minute.

"Stefano, this is Dalia. She is my paralegal and also my girlfriend."

"Ahh" said Stefano, "that is certainly convenient. So, she is forced to spend her entire time with you, day and night. By now, I am certain that she has learned all your secrets and maybe she is ready to move on. Am I correct, *signorina*?"

"*Si deve fare il sacrificio*," said Dalia, with a wisp of a smile, commenting on how one has to make the sacrifice for love.

"Splendid," replied Stefano. "She speaks Italian much better than you, Joe."

"Dalia, this is Stefano Azillo. He is a professor at the law school in Genoa and an old friend of mine. I invited him to lunch to see if he can help us."

Stefano poured them each a glass of Chianti reserve and then looked up at Joe, "And exactly what is this task? You were not so clear on the phone, my old friend."

Joe took a sip of the delicious wine and then cleared his throat. "I am sorry for the mystery but I am operating under strict confidentiality with my client. I am sure you understand. What it comes down to is that we believe there is a new vessel in operation that has a unique means of propulsion called magnetohydrodynamic drive, commonly referred to as MHD. In simple terms, an electric current is passed through seawater in the presence of an intense magnetic field. The interaction of the electric current and the magnet results in the water flowing in one direction, and pushing the ship in the opposite direction. It is unique because there are no moving parts, which makes it silent and reliable."

The professor was obviously taking everything in but still had a confused look on his face. "But Joe, I am a professor of law. How can I help? I am not a scientist."

"Stefano, it is exactly because you are a professor that I need your help. I understand that one of the world's foremost centers for marine engineering is located at the University of Genoa, where you work. It is called DITEN. You are familiar with it."

Chapter 10

"Yes, of course. Everyone is. They occupy the top floors in the building where I have my office."

"Fantastic. What we need is an introduction to someone in that department dealing with MHD design. Just tell them that I represent a potential client who may want to invest in the propulsion system."

Stefano's eyes narrowed as he looked across the table. "And, of course, that is true, my friend?"

"Mostly," replied Barrett sheepishly.

Stefano picked up the near-empty bottle, filled Dalia's glass, and picked at the olives on the platter. "Why don't we order something to eat? I have a feeling we have "mostly" discussed all that we can about your task. I will talk with the department tomorrow. Just don't get me arrested, Joe."

The next morning, Joe checked his emails. Stefano had indeed sent him a message requesting that he meet with Dr. Aldo Gehlardi at the DITEN campus on Via all'Opera Pia before noon. He and Dalia grabbed breakfast in the sunroom on the second floor of the hotel and then walked to the university. The building was fairly modern for Genoa. Unfortunately, its grey concrete facade was uninspiring. They passed through security and took a quick elevator ride to the 5th floor. The two walked down the long hallway reminiscent of most university buildings around the world: functional and worn, with posters and cork boards mounted everywhere. Joe opened the door to Dr. Gehlardi's office and discovered that it had an outer office where his secretary sat. Dalia introduced them to the secretary and noted they had an appointment. The secretary disappeared into the professor's office, and a few minutes later, a very rotund and short man, with a bushy mustache, walked out of the office wearing an old vest, plaid pants, and a shirt with his sleeves rolled up. His glasses were on top of his mostly balding head.

"Welcome to Genoa," he said in flawless English with an American accent. "This morning, Professor Azzilo said very nice things about you and suggested it would be worth my time to spend a few minutes talking with you. Please, come into my office."

"Thank you for taking the time on such short notice," remarked Barrett. "Is that a Boston accent I detect?"

"Yes. Apparently a vestige from my days at MIT."

Joe sat in the guest chair and observed an aging picture on the wall behind the professor. It showed a much younger and fitter Gehlardi leaning on an old but futuristic-looking car with the Boston campus in the background. "Is that a '63 Avanti you are standing next to in the picture?" asked Joe.

"Very astute, Mr. Barrett. That was my favorite car. It was the last model made in the United States by Studebaker. Way ahead of its time."

Both Joe and Dalia then handed the professor their business cards, which he looked at closely.

"Hmm, how is it that I can help two lawyers from New York?" he asked.

Joe smiled and warmly said, "I'm not sure that you can. We are working for a client in the U.K. who has us searching for someone who can help build an MHD propulsion unit for a submarine. I believe it is to be used in offshore drilling fields. But we seem to have exhausted our efforts. Perhaps you can point us to someone who can provide us with such assistance?

"Interesting!" said the professor. "Using MHD in a submersible for commercial purposes. May I ask who your client is?"

Joe responded without missing a beat, "I am sorry, but we have been instructed to keep their name confidential until they decide how to proceed. If you do not feel comfortable talking with us, we understand." Joe shifted in his chair as if he was about to get up.

Dr. Gehlardi stared hard at Joe, but it was clear he was intrigued with the proposal. "Take a seat. No need to leave.

I understand the need for confidentiality, just that this technology is very new and few shipowners know about it."

"Well, I did not say that my client was necessarily a shipowner," said Joe.

"Yes, I see. In any event, I do believe that we have a team of people in our department who have made great strides with magnetic drives, and they may indeed now be functional in a submarine. How big a vessel are you talking about?"

Joe turned to Dalia as if to seek confirmation of the information. He knew this was a tricky question because, if Professor Gehlardi had anything to do with the Pilot Fish, then he might guess the real purpose of their visit if he described the same dimensions. "From what I have been told by my client, he is thinking of more than one submersible. They will probably range from forty feet to maybe eighty feet long."

"And the purpose of the submersibles?"

"My understanding is that they are intended to bring supplies and crew to offshore rigs and drilling sites during bad weather because they can move below the surface. I have also been told that the subs will be used to inspect the wellheads and lines, and they may also be used for seabed inspection as well. It is important that the subs do not create any significant cavitation or noise so as not to interfere with underwater sound receivers and the seismic equipment that are used at those locations for drilling and exploration." Joe had expected the question, and was glad he had done some homework before coming to the meeting. "However, we understand that the science may not be there yet, as the generators necessary to create the electrical impulses in the water would be too large and heavy for a craft the size my client wants to build. So, perhaps we are wasting your time." For a second time, Joe made a motion to get up from his chair. Joe could see that the professor had taken the bait as he motioned Joe to sit back down. "I can assure you, Mr.

Barrett, that the science does exist. You have come to the right place. My team has indeed made several advances in generator capacity and reduction in size. I am confident that an MHD drive can be made available to the size vessels you have suggested. The generator is probably no larger than an American refrigerator. It's just a question of cost. They are extremely expensive to build because of the rare earth materials."

But there are certainly still issues with the design," asked Joe. "I read something about the salinity of water being a problem."

"Yes, in theory, it can be a problem, but we have refined the engine so that it will operate in seawater, which has up to 5 percent salinity. As you know, most of the world's oceans do not exceed 3.5 percent. So, we have not had any problem with salinity in the operation of our design."

Joe let the information sink in, and then asked the critical question, trying to show surprise, "So, you have developed MHD engines for submarines already?"

"Of course," said Azillo, but he quickly added, "however, they are only in a testing stage. I believe my team will soon be prepared to announce that, for a price, we can even manufacture units for underwater vehicles. "

"May I ask the cost of a unit developing, say, five thousand horse-power?"

"That is a large unit, Mr. Barrett. Your client must be transporting very heavy equipment."

"Well, there is also the issue of speed. To cut down on the expense of delays, my client is hoping that the submersibles can also achieve at least thirty knots speed."

The professor's secretary entered the room and signaled in the direction of his phone. It was clear that he had another commitment.

"Yes, that would not be a problem. Well, I think that is about all I can say for the moment, Mr. Barrett. If your client wants to meet with me and my team, we will be pleased to set it up."

"Thank you. Dr. Gehlardi. But you were about to give us an indication of the cost. That is obviously critical to my client's decision."

"More than fifty million U.S. dollars, Mr. Barrett. Now if you will excuse me. I have another meeting." The change in the professor's voice made it clear that he was finished talking.

Dalia and Joe both rose from their seats, shook the rotund professor's large hand, and headed into the hallway. As they walked towards the elevator, Joe put his finger up to his lips, signaling Dalia not to talk until they got out of the building.

CHAPTER 11
GENOA

Inside Dr. Gehlardi's office, the secretary pointed to the blinking light on the telephone sitting at the edge of his desk. He looked once more at the phone number of the person calling and then lifted the handset. "Pronto?" Over the next two minutes, the academic's face became increasingly worried and upset.

"You should have called me a half-hour ago, before I met with them. How was I to know who they were?' There was a pause, and then, rubbing his forehead, he replied on the phone, "I did not give them any useful information. We just talked about the possibility of MHD propulsion. He seems to know a lot about it. They would not tell me who their client is." The professor then listened some more, taking the time to wipe his huge head with a handkerchief from his pocket. It was clear that he was now getting annoyed.

"Look, you do whatever you want to do with them. Leave me out of it. You can't hide this science forever. It's my invention, and I am not going to go through life with the plans locked in a safe. You paid me well, but not that well." The professor slammed the phone down. "Stunod," he said, and reached into his drawer for an antacid.

Out on the street, Joe looked over his shoulder several times to see if anyone was following them. "I think we found our source for the engine. Not sure what happened at the end, though."

Chapter 11

"He got a call," said Dalia. "I saw the hold-light on his phone blinking. I don't think it was someone he wanted to speak to."

"Let's hope the call was not about us. Now, the question is, how do we find out who hired him to develop this technology?"

Dalia immediately went into her "solution mode." Ever since Joe met her, he had been amazed how she came up with inventive ideas on how to get around impossible situations. She had suggested once that they play janitors in a hospital to get into a guarded room where two children were held hostage. The amazing thing was that the idea actually worked.

"OK," she said. "We return tomorrow to thank Professor Azolli for introducing us to the engineering department. Only thing is that, once we are in the building, you visit your law professor friend on the second floor, and I stop by Dr. Gehlardi's office on the fifth floor. We have to wait until about one o'clock when everyone in Genoa goes home to have lunch. I'll tell the guard on the floor that I left my phone in his office. I suspect he'll remain with me after opening the office. I'll stand behind him and put some tape on the door lock. Then, I conveniently find my phone. He will insist on taking me back into the hallway. But when he leaves, I head back to Dr. Gehlardi's office, open the door, and get into his secretary's computer. I doubt I can get into the professor's private office as it has its own lock. Hopefully, after a quick review of the computer files, I'll find something." She put her hand on her hips, smiled, and then winked at Joe. "How's that?" Joe grinned and responded, "That has to be the craziest idea I have ever heard."

"Worked on NCIS," she shrugged. "You got a better plan?" Dalia loved watching television shows with her son, and seemed to have a photographic memory of the storylines.

"For this afternoon, sure. We take a ride down to Portofino and I'll show you a view to die for." He grabbed her hand and they headed off for the car.

Chapter 12
Portofino

Portofino is one of those places that appears in many bucket lists. At the end of a peninsula called Punta Chiappa, just south of Genoa, it is the setting for a quaint fishing village famous for its picturesque harbor filled with small fishing boats and glamorous yachts bobbing in turquoise-blue water. The colorful buildings that nestle down to the edge of the water holds expensive shops or restaurants on the first floor, with apartments above that are equally expensive. There is even an underground garage where everyone is required to park their car. It's located at the entrance to the town so as to maintain a quaint appearance in the village center.

Joe and Dalia sat at an open table at a restaurant called Estrella di Notte, only a few feet from the edge of the town docks where a number of very impressive motor yachts were tied up. They dined on figs and cheese, thin slices of octopus over arugula, a classic penne é pesto, and finally, a whole branzino fish. Joe selected a wonderful Vermentino wine that was harvested in Cinque Terra, a mountainous land mass just across the bay. They spoke cautiously of their future plans, and circumvented the word marriage, but they both knew it was inevitable.

As Joe took a final sip of grappa, he leaned over and kissed Dalia. Then, he whispered in her ear, "Don't look to your left, but there is a man over there, blue sport jacket, black t-shirt, who has been watching us all evening. I think he has even taken some nice photos of us with his phone."

"What do you suggest we do?" said Dalia, without any hint of nervousness in her voice.

"Why don't we introduce ourselves?" said Joe. He waved the waiter down and paid the bill. Then, the two got up and walked arm-in-arm along the cobblestone street towards the garage, which would lead them right past the table with the mysterious man. Joe pretended to be a bit drunk and wobbly on his feet. He made a couple of loud comments that were slurred. As they approached the table, the mystery man in the blue sport jacket looked away, trying to avoid eye contact. Joe stopped inches from the table, and suddenly whirled around on his toes, with his hands outstretched, calling out, "Magnifico!" Then, Joe promptly lost balance and fell on top of the man who was still seated. His chair fell backward, and Joe found himself lying in a comical, if not potentially embarrassing, position directly over the middle-aged and brawny male. The two men looked at each other with their eyes so close that Joe had to close one eye to keep his vision in focus.

Barrett picked himself up while apologizing for his drinking, and brushed the dust off the jacket shoulder of the obviously annoyed male. "*Scuzzi, Scuzzi,*" he kept repeating with the fake slur. The man pushed him back, his face full of anger. Joe apologized once more, and then he turned and walked away. He took Dalia by the arm and headed towards the garage. Once they were out of sight of the table, Joe opened his hand and revealed that he had taken the man's cell phone.

"Quick," said Joe. "Follow me. He will discover his phone is missing in another minute." Barrett turned left onto a narrow alleyway between two buildings. The alley was dark and without lights. At the end stood a church on a small piazza. Joe hurried towards the church. Dalia thought they were going to seek refuge in the chapel, but instead, Joe kept up the jog and soon they were in a forest behind the old stone sanctuary. Somewhere far behind them, they could hear a man shouting. They assumed the mystery man discovered that his cell phone was gone. Joe looked at Dalia with the "trust-me" face and kept going further into the forest, down a narrow but worn path that worked its way up the high hill.

Joe kept walking but spoke loudly enough for Dalia to hear. "I'm betting he is going to the garage to look for us. When he can't find us there, he will start looking elsewhere. There are dozens of hiking trails through the national forest on Punta Chiappa that are used mostly by the local people. We are on a small one that goes to the next village, Paraggi. If we're lucky, he won't know about these trails. If he does, we have about a five or ten-minute head start on him. This path is a couple of miles long."

"And when we get to Paraggi, then what?"

"Well, the last time I took this path it ended at a small parking lot. Lots of cars. You can pick your color and style."

"I am beginning to believe you are crazy," Dalia responded. "Hey, I'm not the one putting tape on door locks."

They forged on at a brisk pace, using the phone as a flashlight. In the distance, they could see the lights of Cinque Terra and the fishing boats anchored in the bay.

"I must say, Joe, you really know how to charm a girl on such a warm and beautiful night in the heart of a romantic fishing village. Can't remember the last date I was on when we had to run through the forest to get away from a killer." As she finished the sentence, there was a wild and raw shriek followed by grunting in front of them. "What was that?" Dalia said, for the first time a bit scared.

"Hmm, my guess is that was a wild boar and her family. They are all around here. They can be nasty. Don't frighten them."

"Don't frighten them? Are you kidding? How about me? We don't have wild boars in Astoria, Queens." Joe suddenly stopped, noticing a flash of small shadows that ran across the path in front of them and into the underbrush.

The path finally descended, and they could see the dim lights of a parking lot. "How do we know the guy isn't waiting for us in the parking lot?" said Dalia.

"We don't, but it looks like there are only about a half dozen cars in the lot. There is no security. Let's go for the old Honda in the back. You like dark blue, right?" Joe quietly moved towards the car in the dirt-covered lot. He took his jacket off, wrapped it around his elbow, and pulled his arm back, instinctively turning his head away from the glass side window.

"Ahh, Mr. Bond, before you do that, may I suggest you try opening the door? The door isn't locked."

Joe looked back at the door and saw the button on the side window was in the up position. He gently pulled the door handle and the car door swung open. Dalia laughed, covering her mouth. They quickly got in the car and looked for the keys. If the door was not locked, the odds were that the driver left the keys in the car. Sure enough, he found the key fob in the cup holder between the front seats. Two seconds later, the car was started and they slowly edged out of the parking lot. Joe told Dalia to crouch down in the seat – if anyone was looking for them, they would be searching for a car with a man and a woman in the front seats. The car exited onto the narrow, winding, two-lane road that ran to the mainland. As they proceeded along at a moderate speed, with no cars behind them, it occurred to Joe that they could not go back to their hotel. The mystery man, if he had been following them, probably knew they were staying at the Bristol Hotel. After about three miles, the Honda slowly entered the town of Santa Margherita. Scores of tourists crossed the street to the beach and the marina. Joe pulled into a side street near the end of the town and parked behind a bank building. He shut off the car lights and then pulled the man's phone out of his pocket. Fortunately, the phone had been left unlocked. They quickly searched through the photos. Sure enough, there were a string of photos of Joe and Dalia coming out of their hotel in Genoa, having lunch, walking into the university building, and later, coming out. The last photos were of them driving to Portofino and eating at the restaurant.

"Well, finally we have some photos to bring home about our vacation. And it looks like we're going to have to find another place for tonight. There is a small hotel at the end of this road. Let's stay there. It's definitely out of the way." As Joe maneuvered the car into the Hotel Suisse, Dalia scrolled through the text messages, emails, and contact list.

"Joe, we've got problems. This guy has been following us for days, and he's reporting to someone in Korea whose text name is Geulimja. I just looked that up on Google. It means shadow." She scrolled down further on the phone. It's not clear why he is tracking us, but the messages have a tone to them that I don't like. Also, there's a couple of emails to the Bei Mei company in China that don't make sense. Remember, that's the company connected to North Korea and to Hong Shipping?"

"Why don't you upload that stuff to Tim in New York and let him follow up on this stuff. We've had enough excitement for one day." Joe parked in the back of the hotel, remembered to lock the car with the keys, and headed to the hotel. Without any luggage, he could only guess what the lady at check-in was thinking as they asked for a room for the night.

The next morning, they timed the arrival at the DITEN campus for exactly one p.m. Joe was worried that the police would spot their Honda as stolen, but apparently, it had not yet been reported as missing. Meanwhile, Joe also called the car rental agency and requested they pick up the Fiat from the garage in Portofino.

They both walked into the building together and announced they were there to see Professor Azillo. After entering the elevator, Joe got off on the second floor while Dalia continued to the fifth. As expected, the offices were nearly all empty as everyone had taken their lunch break, which was closer to a siesta. Dalia tried the door to Gehlardi's office, but it was locked. She quietly walked down the hallway until she found an old man dressed in a simple guard's uniform. He was sleeping in his chair. Dalia spoke loudly enough to wake the man and told a story about how she thought she had left her cell phone in Professor's Gehlardi's office that morning. The old guard seemed amused by the pretty young woman's plea and walked to the office door while searching for the key on his chain. "Ecco," he said, and with that, opened the door. Just as Dalia had predicted, the guard insisted on coming into the secretary's office to watch. Dalia pointed to something on the floor next to the waiting room chair. While the old man tried to focus his vision on the floor area, Dalia immediately slapped the clear tape over the latch to the doorframe. As she walked slowly through the room, she held her phone tightly in her hand, out of sight of the guard. Suddenly, she stopped and did a small pirouette and bent over to the table. Dalia stood up straight, smiling, and holding her hand out with the phone in the direction of the security man. The guard turned and grinned, and then complimented her good fortune. They then walked out of the office.

Dalia hoped the guard would not notice the tape or the lack of a click of the lock as the door shut. The elderly watchman, however, was focused on putting his long chain of keys back in his pocket. They jingled like wind chimes. The guard then escorted Dalia back to the elevator bank where he bid her good day as he pressed the button for the lift.

Chapter 12

The elevator, thankfully, took some time to arrive. By then, the guard had gone back to his chair around the corner. Dalia quietly walked back to Dr. Gehlardi's office where she very gently turned the door handle and held her breath that the lock had not closed. There was a low squeak as the door pushed in. Dalia quickly pulled off the tape and stepped into the office, and then closed the door behind her. She looked at her phone. It was 1:18 p.m. Joe had sent a text saying, "Are u in? hurry up." She just responded "y."

Thank goodness the secretary had left her computer on so it did not have to reboot. The home screen had an icon for "Gehlardi clients." She clicked and a screen immediately came up asking for the password. Dalia had not thought about this problem. She looked around the desk and in the desk drawers for a piece of paper with the password. No luck. Then, she picked up the keyboard, and afterward, looked under the phone. Still nothing. She tried typing in the secretary's name, displayed on a brass plate fastened to the front of the desk. Dalia suspected that would be a pretty stupid password. A red warning came up that the wrong password had been entered, and after two more attempts, the computer would be shut down. Then, she tried the name of the institute, DITEN, but again, the red warning light flashed. One more try before the system locked her out. The word obviously had to be something personal to the Professor. Then, she remembered Joe making much of the picture on Gehlardi's wall, and typed in "63Avanti." With a *whirr* and a buzz, the screen opened up. She was into his files.

With a grin, Dalia scrolled down the lists. All the files looked very technical. Then, she saw the one file name that was out of place: *ombra*, the Italian word for shadow. Dalia remembered it was also used in the communication by the strange man with the Chinese company. Dalia double-clicked on the file name and a moment later it opened up. Bingo. There were the plans for the MHD and email communications with "shadow." She highlighted the communications and then sent them as an email to her Gmail account. It seemed to take ages. As soon as it went through, she erased the sent email and then the deleted email before closing out the computer.

At the same moment, Dalia froze as she heard a woman standing in front of the office door talking to someone else. If that was the professor's secretary, she would be caught. There was nowhere to hide in the small vestibule area. She stood motionless near the door. It was definitely the secretary's voice, and a second later, she heard the key go into the lock. But it was just as quickly pulled out without being turned. From what she could hear, the secretary had decided to head to the ladies room to freshen up. Dalia waited a half minute and then slowly opened the door. She peeked down the hallway. Someone had come out of the elevator but turned in the opposite direction. Dalia quietly closed the door behind her and briskly walked to the lift. A moment later, she was inside the elevator and headed down towards the lobby. On her way out, she typed a quick text telling Joe she was about to leave the building.

As Dalia stepped out of the elevator on the ground floor she saw Dr. Gehlardi standing only a few feet away in front of the adjoining elevator. His back was toward her and he stared at the floor, in a deep conversation with two other men. Dalia quickly turned her back towards him and walked out of the elevator towards the lobby door. She could hear the professor pause to cough, and then he went back into his conversation. He entered the elevator without ever looking up.

Dalia sent Joe a quick text to warn him to be careful that Dr. Gehlardi was in the north side elevator cab and was heading back to his office. Joe was, in fact, at the elevator doors waiting for an elevator when he saw the message. Professor Azillo stuck out his hand to push the single call button on the wall when Joe grabbed Stefano's hand and began shaking it. "I really appreciate what you did for me, Stefano. I think the client is going to be very interested in working with Dr. Gehlardi's team. He has done some fascinating work."

Professor Azillo was a bit surprised by the awkward moment but just smiled. "Joe, just remember next time to bring that lovely woman with you. She definitely brings out the best in you. Ciao, my friend. I hope to see you in New York the next time I visit."

Joe pushed the call button, seeing that the first elevator was now on the fifth floor, and was not moving. Two seconds later, the second cab stopped at his floor and Joe waved to Professor Azillo. His heart was pumping fast. When he got to the lobby, he quickly headed for the doors and then turned into the parking lot. Dalia was already in the car and talking on the cell phone. When Joe opened the door, he heard her talking with Captain Ken about having forwarded the email to her account. Dalia was amazingly calm. She described some of the emails she had spotted. It sounded like Dr. Gehlardi was sending a lot of information to North Korea about his work with the MHD.

Joe got the car started and they were on the highway headed north in minutes. He figured it was best to avoid the airport at Milan in case Gehlardi discovered the hacking of his computer and alerted the police, or worse, sent the mysterious man to find them. Joe decided to drive to the airport in Geneva, Switzerland. That would take about five hours. Leaving Italy would not be a problem since there were no longer border guards. However, Barrett remembered that their luggage and clothing were still back at the Bristol Hotel. He would have to arrange for their bags to be shipped back to New York.

Joe was sorry that Dalia never had a real chance to see the area around Liguria. Well, on their next trip, they would spend some real vacation time in Italy, assuming the Italian government allowed them back in.

Chapter 13
Pyongyang

The young dictator was furious. He had spent millions of hard-to-get U.S. dollars on the submarine. This unknown American lawyer had thwarted every effort he had made to get the sub back, interfering with his project and costing him millions, just when he was on the verge of making history. He slammed a cup down on the table, shattering the fine porcelain. It had been a gift from the Chinese government to his father. They would give him another one. Everyone was in fear of the young man. For a moment, his mood softened and he chuckled. His father had taught him to be crazy like a rabid fox. "Everyone will avoid you," he had said, "No one wants to catch the disease."

But, just as quickly, his mood soured. The imperialists had blocked almost all of his efforts to obtain foreign currency, which he needed to pay for the rocket motors for his intercontinental missles. He had found a factory in Dnipro, a town in the Ukraine, which still had the plans for the old Soviet rockets, including the giant SS-18. Still, he needed money. His latest plan to get foreign currency was to enter the drug market. It seemed like a foolproof strategy. He would sell Chinese opium to the Western world and watch them suffer while reaping the profits. A year ago, the young chairman had come up with a new idea. He would build two submersibles that could not only be used to smuggle drugs and money, but eventually would also be the perfect vehicles to deliver his atomic bombs to key cities in the U.S. without worrying about whether the rockets could be accurately navigated or survive re-entry. His scientists told him they were always on the verge of solving the technical problems with the missiles, but progress was a lot slower than they predicted. The beauty of his plan was that, while everyone was watching the sky, his submarines could quietly enter an American port, hidden under a large commercial freighter. The subs could access the harbors of New York, Long Beach, New Orleans, and Norfolk without anyone ever knowing. When the bombs went off, the greatest American cities would burn for years. The best part was that the Americans would not be able to launch a counter-attack because they would not know who exploded the bombs.

It was, indeed, a brilliant plan. But now it was falling apart as the inept old man Hong allowed one of his submersibles to be discovered and taken by the British. Meanwhile, this American spy, Barrett, was interfering with every effort by the dictator to get the sub back or have it destroyed. More worrisome was that Barrett was obviously putting the puzzle together. Soon, he would realize that the North Korean government was behind the submersible and what its true purpose was.

The young dictator went into another rage. Why had the shadow failed to eliminate the American? He was told only that something had gone wrong in Italy, and that the messenger's team had lost contact with Barrett. How difficult was it to shoot the spy? Time was running out. The U.N. embargoes were taking their toll on his country, and the Chinese were suddenly not being so cooperative with his government. They were beginning to suspect something about the real purpose of the subs. *The idiots*, he thought. They built the submersibles for him at their secret government yard. In exchange, the Chinese were to get the plans for the MHD drive, which the dictator had constructed with the help of some very expensive research done in Italy.

The Chinese had been given bits and pieces of blueprints and drawings at a trickle pace; the chubby tyrant knew full well that once the Chinese had obtained the complete plan for the magnetohydrodynamic drive, that would be the last assistance he would receive from them.

He scribbled a note on a piece of paper and handed it to the young lieutenant, who was his secretary. The junior officer looked at the note, which simply said "Kill Barrett." He dutifully placed the folded note into a leather briefcase and marched in military step out of the Chairman's office.

Chapter 14
New York

The view out of Joe's office on the thirty-fourth floor was not spectacular. There were a lot of buildings, short and tall, which seemed to be within a hand's reach, and they all effectively prevented any clear view of the horizon, the street, or the sky. A sliver of the East River could be seen by cocking his head to the right and squinting one eye while standing near the wall. Joe was reassured by his partners that the rare and difficult sight gave him an upscale office, which was classified by the firm as having a "water view." Joe spent little time looking out the four-foot-wide window, and situated his desk so that he immediately confronted anyone who entered his office.

Everyone in the law firm had their office walls done in standard Benjamin Moore antique white. Joe felt that a rather dull color and took matters into his own hands, literally. He painted his walls a distintive green color politely described as "celadon," after also painting his apartment bathroom with the same color. Not having enough paint to cover the last wall, he decided that a maroon color, which was on sale by the quart at a local hardware store, was perfect for completing the job. While the senior partners had initially raised hell about the painted walls in Barrett's office, secretly, many of the junior lawyers were jealous they had not done the same thing, albeit with perhaps a better eye for the color wheel. In the end, Joe was allowed to keep the color paint on the wall, as that would be far easier than letting him organize a revolution for the younger lawyers.

Joe was sitting up straight at his desk in the Audubon wing chair he had salvaged from a tag sale. His tie was removed and his shirt sleeves loosely rolled up. He thumped his index finger on the memo in front of him. Ken, Tim, and Dalia sat across from him on uncoordinated guest chairs uncertain where the conversation was going. "I'm telling you the Pilot Fish is being coordinated out of North Korea, and yes, I think their government is behind it. The question is why? What do they intend to use the sub for? I don't believe it is just for selling drugs." Joe looked at his staff and paused, waiting to be challenged.

"Joe, we all probably agree with you. But there is no smoking gun," replied Captain Ken in his very calm, resonating voice. "We can't just tell London that our best hunch is that the vessel is being controlled by the North Koreans without some real evidence. The East of London Insurance company may not laugh, but they won't take us seriously. More importantly, if it is a diplomatic issue, they have to convince the British government that this is more than the hunch of some New York lawyers."

"OK," replied Barrett, "Let's say I agree with you. What is the evidence, the smoking gun that we need to convince the Brits?" His question was met with deadly silence and a lot of heads looking down. Finally, Tim looked up and said, "If Hong Line was located in North Korea, that would have made it easy."

"That's it," Joe said. "We have to focus on the connection between Hong's company and the North Koreans. Dalia has already uncovered a lot of stuff about their carrying coal from China to North Korea, but we need more. Dalia, you said that Hong must be borrowing a lot of money to keep his ships in service. Maybe he is borrowing it from North Korea?"

CHAPTER 14

"Actually, that's a pretty good theory. I will start working on that angle today," she replied.

"But we still don't know what the grand plan is for the sub," commented Tim.

Dalia finally looked up, her green eyes opened wide, signaling she had thought up another crazy plan. Joe sat back in his seat. He had a feeling this was going to be a wild one.

"Well, gentleman, I think the best way to uncover whatever is going on at the Hong Line is to speak with Mr. Hong himself. The Pilot Fish is not a plot at some low level. It is far too expensive, illegal, and militant to be run by some clerks or employees at the lower level of the company. I would confront Mr. Hong with the facts we have developed so far and see how he reacts. Tell him we know about the drugs and the money, and that we know he is planning something far larger with the vehicle. He is either going to bluff, bargain, or intimidate. Either way, he reveals his hand, and he will most likely have to accelerate whatever been has planned. I suspect someone is building another Pilot Fish. We pass the word to the American and British government and let them do the field work to find the ship."

Ken leaned back in deep thought and finally uttered, "And what if he already has another Pilot Fish, or perhaps even more? Maybe we just lit the fuse on something that was calm and quiet."

"Good point, Ken. But if we do nothing, Hong is in full control of this mystery project. If we force his hand, maybe he will make a mistake. I say we try Dalia's idea. Mike Graham can lean on Hong's insurance company to demand that Hong give us a meeting. He must know the underwriters are investigating the incident. If he refuses, the insurance company will threaten to cut off his coverage. He can't sail his ships into most ports of the world without insurance. He'll cooperate. I'll call Mike and ask that he arrange a meeting with Hong."

As the others got up and left his room, Joe adjusted his chair so that he could look out the window. Squinting his right eye, he could just see a garbage scow being pushed by a tug effortlessly down the East River. A moment later, it was gone. Joe picked up the phone and called London.

Chapter 15
Astoria

That evening, Joe helped with the dishes after a wonderful dinner that Dalia cooked from a family recipe. Her mother, Farah, had taken Daniel, her son, earlier that day to see relatives in New Jersey. They were not expected to return until tomorrow.

Joe scooped more suds onto the plates in an effort to get them spotless and felt Dalia's arms encircle his waist and her warm breath moving up the back of his neck. Barrett grinned and squirmed. He was always slightly embarrassed when Dalia showed him affection in her home because others shared the house. But his relationship with Dalia had moved far beyond friendship. He would propose to her and that, interestingly, did not frighten him at all. Now near forty, the time had come to settle down. He actually was looking forward to coming home to his own family.

"Don't tell me I have left the great Joe Barrett speechless!" said Dalia, as she pressed her body up against his back so that he could feel her swollen breasts. She then slowly rotated her pelvis. Her hands carefully tussled his curly hair, and she planted a long and wet kiss on the side of his neck.

He gently put down the last dish and then bent his knees and twisted his torso so that her hands unlocked. He maneuvered his arms behind her head and pulled her closer towards his face. The kiss was breathtaking, warm, and slow, sending a chill up Dalia's spine. Finally, Joe let go, using the tip of his index finger to plant a large bubble of dish soap from his hands on Dalia's nose. Not to be outdone, Dalia giggled, crossed her beautiful bottle-green eyes, and stuck out her tongue as she swiveled her head back and forth to dislodge the white suds from her nose. Her ponytail struggled to keep up with her gyrations. Suddenly, Dalia became quiet, staring down at the floor. Once again, she held him tight, her arms clasping at his back and her head buried in his shoulder. He knew instantly that something was troubling her.

"Joe, I'm scared. Frightened. I am worried that you, we, have gotten in way over our heads on this case. The man following us in Italy may be just the beginning and we don't know what he was intending to do. I still remember the pictures of us on his phone. We're not equipped to take on bad guys. Let someone else do it."

She quietly stood back a foot or so and looked slowly up at him with a very serious face. "What I'm really saying is that I don't want you to get hurt… I just don't want to lose you. Promise me you won't do something… stupid, OK?"

He saw a tear forming in her right eye and knew she was, indeed, scared. Anyone would be, but perhaps her family's history brought out the fear in her. Her mother was Lebanese and her father was born in Italy. The family moved from Beirut to Marseilles when the crisis in Lebanon was too much to endure. Dalia was still a small girl when they arrived in France; she had few memories of Beirut other than the beautiful white beaches that seemed to come up to the doorsteps of the tall and classic buildings that looked out over the Mediterranean Sea. Life in Europe was far calmer than the Middle East, but not without its toll. She was told at age fourteen that her father died mysteriously on a business trip, but when she got older, Dalia suspected that he had been killed by one of the terrorist groups based in Lebanon for not cooperating in some illicit trade.

Joe held back his normal instinct to make a joke, and instead reached out once more and held her closely. They were both in love and would do anything to protect the other. Joe used his hand to gently push the wisps of chestnut hair off her face where they were sticking to the wet cheeks. Softly, he assured her that he would not do anything stupid and that she could always count on him being at her side. She leaned her head back and stared closely into his face, then put her finger to her lips and led him by the hand to the bedroom. There would be no more talk of bad guys tonight.

As the light in the upstairs bedroom flicked off, a dark-colored Honda sat across the street. The driver, with his jet-black hair and loose black clothing, could hardly be seen. His expensive Nikon camera, which had a night-vision lens, rested on the passenger seat. A blue light glowed from the seat as the cell phone vibrated, its ringer shut off. The man leaned over and cautiously held the phone to his mouth, covering it with his other hand so that the light from the screen could not be seen outside the car. He whispered into the phone, grunting, and showing displeasure with the instruction he had just been given. He was told not to do the job in the house; they didn't want the girl involved. Too bad, he thought, as he looked at the satchel of deadly toys he had brought with him. The wicked-looking *geom*, a single-handed and slightly curved sword with a leather handle, was wrapped in a silk sheet and waiting on the back seat. The young man had spent hours getting just the right edge on the exquisite steel blade that was forged over a century ago in Korea. He reminded himself that patience was the greatest virtue of an assassin. With a crooked smile, he started the car and quietly drove away with the headlights off. The car disappeared within seconds into the inky darkness of the night, helped in part by two street lamps that had mysteriously gone out. Their bulbs had been smashed earlier by two small shuriken that had been expertly thrown by the driver.

As the car disappeared into the night, a curtain closed a couple of inches on the second floor window of a dark apartment diagonally across the street from Dalia's home. Inside, an elderly Syrian woman named Amena left the dark bedroom and went down to the kitchen. She looked worried. She had been through enough wars in her homeland to know that the dark car with the hard-to-see man inside was trouble. Tomorrow, she would tell her friend Farah what had happened. That was what neighbors were for, and that was how neighbors survived. You had to watch each other's back.

Chapter 16
Manhattan

The pre-trial conference before Judge Nizzo in the Manhattan federal court was conducted without any surprises. The judge was focused on when the parties could complete their exchange of documents and finish taking the depositions of dozens of witnesses so that there would be enough evidence to order the attorneys before a magistrate in an effort to mediate a settlement. Daniel Nizzo had been on the bench long enough to know that there was no point starting settlement talks until the parties had all the evidence. The problem was getting the lawyers, or their clients, to turn over the relevant documents and materials in their files. For that, he used the power of his office, and his voice, threatening sanctions against those parties who were delaying production and complimenting those who had cooperated. When the hearing ended, he stood up from his bench desk to the sound of a dozen lawyers in the courtroom also simultaneously standing as a courtesy to the judge.

Nizzo closed the thick file involving a ship that had caught fire at sea. He was impressed that the shipowner's lawyer, Mr. Barrett, had not put on his usual display of witticism and jocularity for which he was well known in the courthouse. The judge suspected that Barrett's history of banter was usually a clever diversion for some shortcoming in respect to his client's case, but the judge had to admit that, today, Barrett had been subdued and professional throughout the conference. Perhaps the man had changed. The attorneys left the courtroom as soon as Judge Nizzo passed through the robing room doors.

As they were descending the steps in front of the courthouse, Ken grabbed Joe by the elbow to stop him. "Joe, I have to go back into the courthouse. I was at the marine store on Chambers Street this morning picking up some stuff for my boat. They made me leave it with the security desk. It'll only take a second."

"OK, but I am going to head onto the subway station. Probably meet you there on the platform, but if a train comes in, I want to get back to the office."

"Everything all right, Joe? You seemed a bit quiet during the court conference."

"Yeah. Just that Dalia's a bit worried about some things, and I don't know how to assure her that everything is fine."

"Wrong subject for me to provide advice, Joe. I'm divorced. Obviously, I didn't say the right things the first time around. Anyway, catch up with you in a moment."

Captain Ken turned around and bounded up the stairs to the front doors of the federal courthouse. Joe continued on at a slow pace, heading towards Centre Street. The entrance to the subway station was on the corner. He carefully descended the steps, getting a whiff of some potent smells.

The Brooklyn Bridge-City Hall subway station, about three blocks long underground, was one of the oldest in New York. It was "lightly" refurbished by the city a decade ago but the tiles on the floor and the walls were mostly stained and dirty. Steel I-beam pillars, painted in shiny black and only a foot wide, were spaced continuously along the platform to support the old cement ceiling. The indirect fluorescent lighting was, at best, adequate. At rush hour, the station was packed with people who worked at City Hall, the Municipal Building, the police headquarters, and, of course, the courthouses; but in the early afternoon, the station was often very quiet, with only stray passengers seeking a subway ride.

Chapter 16

Joe went through the turnstile and headed towards the Green Line's uptown platform. Fifty feet behind him, a wiry man followed. He was dressed in a black hooded sweatshirt, dark sweatpants, and rubber-soled shoes. He was carrying over his shoulder a leather tube used by artists to transport their paintings. His face could not be seen under the hood, but strands of thick black hair peeked out from the covering.

Both the express and the local trains were leaving the station as Barrett reached the bottom of the stairs and stepped onto the empty platform. He walked over to where the third car normally stopped on the local side, knowing that when he got off the train, he would be directly in front of the exit to that station. Barrett then took out his cell phone to check for messages. He was surprised to see a voice mail and a text from Dalia's mother, Farah, asking that he call her immediately.

Joe sensed something over his right shoulder. As he turned, he could see the glint of light reflected off a polished and slightly curved blade that was raised straight up in the air. The sword, about three feet long, was perfectly still and pointed at the ceiling. The man holding it was difficult to see under the long hood, but his features were definitely Asian. His eyes were focused on Joe.

"What the hell?" said Barrett, as he watched the young man adjust his left leg forward. With a double grip, the samurai sword came down with lightning speed. Joe instinctively twisted and brought his briefcase up in front of his head. The thin blade whistled through the air, narrowly missing Joe's right hand, and sliced through the heavy leather case as if it were butter. The bag split wide open and one end fell to the ground. Shredded paper fell out from the remainder of the briefcase that was still in Joe's hand. Bits and pieces of a legal pad fluttered to the floor. The attacker just smiled.

Barrett threw what was left of his briefcase at his assailant, who easily ducked while the sliced bag skidded over the floor tiles. Joe quickly turned his head and saw there was no one else in the station. There was no point in screaming for help. As the assassin once more raised his double-fisted sword, Joe was injected with a rush of adrenaline. He sprinted to the nearest pillar as the assassin followed. Barrett looked at the cell phone in his hand. He punched in 911 with his thumb and dropped the phone on the floor.

"Why are you trying to kill me?" he yelled, hoping that his voice would be heard by the operator over the phone. "If you want my wallet or my watch, take it."

The assailant still wore an amused expression on his face and refused to respond. He feinted to the left and then to the right, less than ten feet from the pillar, to see what Joe would do. Then, he grunted as if he were about to attack, but pulled back. It was obvious he was enjoying the game. With another incredibly fast movement, the attacker brought the blade down millimeters from one edge of the steel support. Joe turned his body away towards the other side. The blade caught the sleeve of his suit and neatly removed a few inches of the pin-striped fabric, leaving a sliver of a cut along his wrist. Joe looked again at the man and saw him grin. It was obvious that the next attack would come from the other side of the narrow pillar. The steel beam provided too little cover.

Joe slowly crouched with his hands over his head, looking like a young child trying to hide in the open. The move confused the attacker for a moment, and Barrett used the split second to sprint towards the display for the subway map that was about twenty feet away. The six-foot billboard was floor to ceiling and made of steel. It provided a lot more cover than the pillar. Just as he reached out for the frame, Joe felt a burning pain in his right shoulder. The wound surprised him. He lost his step, tripped, and fell on his knees to the platform. With his left hand, he reached over his shoulder and pulled out two small stars made of steel. They had pierced through his jacket and shirt and lodged under his skin. Blood was on the tips of each metal object. He threw them on the floor.

Rolling over and looking up, Barrett could see the figure of the attacker only a couple of steps away. His smirk had disappeared and his eyes had narrowed on the caged victim. With both hands, he again raised his ancient sword, steadying his stance, obviously getting ready for the kill. All Joe could do was bring his arm up to protect his face. His last thought was that he regretted having doubted Dalia. Joe heard a loud swooshing sound and closed his eyes. Nothing happened. Joe opened one eye and saw the assassin still poised with the sword over his head, but the man was frozen, staring at the ceiling. Strangely, there was a searing sound and the smell of burned flesh. Then, the assailant fell forward, face first, landing stiffly on the concrete platform. The sword, still in his grip, stuck the platform only inches from Joe's head. Barrett was surprised to see that the back of the assailant's sweatshirt was charred and on fire. Bright yellow sparks flew out from the center of his back like the end of a roman candle.

"Joe are you OK. Are you injured?" Ken leaned over Joe and grabbed him by the elbow. Shouts came from both ends of the platform, and they heard heavy boots running on cement. Joe opened both eyes and saw Ken standing to his side, loosely holding an orange-colored plastic gun in his right hand. Joe looked at Ken quizzically and nodded at the gun.

"Oh, that. It's an emergency flare gun. I bought it at the marine store with some other stuff for my boat. That's why they wouldn't let me in the courthouse with the shopping bag. I had to leave it with the security desk. Guess it was a good thing it came with two flare shells when I bought it. By the way, you owe me a replacement shell." Joe grinned and got to his feet. He put his hand over the punctures in his shoulder and noticed that there was still a little blood on his fingers.

"Well, here come the police. I guess they may have some questions. I suspect we won't be going back to the office this afternoon," commented Ken. "By the way, good thing he attacked you here. The video surveillance camera is right overhead, and there is another one over there. That should clear us with the police."

Joe used his hands to brush off his suit and straighten his tie as the first of the policemen arrived. He looked at the two halves of his briefcase lying on the platform. "I think we need to raise our fee rate for Mike. We just earned hazard pay."

Chapter 17
New York

"I don't exactly know what this case is about that your team is working on, Joe, but frankly I think it involves risks that our firm would not normally handle. Having said that, I am not going to stop you, mostly because I know you. You would quit your job here before letting a file go unfinished. Admirable, in some ways, but won't do you much good if you get killed."

Joe sat across from Mr. McDonald, the senior Managing Partner, with a bandage around his wrist and thought about events of the past few days. He and Ken kept their story simple: They had no idea who the man was that attacked Joe and no reason to know why the attack took place. They simply treated the attacker as some sort of a crazy man. One of the detectives had revealed that the assailant's identity could not be determined. There were no government records on him. His fingerprints were not on file.

When Joe was pressed by the police about what work he was involved in at the law firm, he gave details about some of the actual lawsuits that he was handling. He mentioned in passing about doing an investigation for a London marine insurance company, and thankfully no one bothered to follow up. Joe and Ken both knew the assailant had something to do with the Pilot Fish. Obviously, someone in Korea, north or south, had stepped up the pressure to get to Joe.

Joe smiled to himself, knowing that the attack meant his investigation was obviously going in the right direction. Somewhere, he was touching a raw nerve.

"Joe, are you feeling OK? You haven't responded." Mr. McDonald rose from his chair. Joe thought fleetingly about his torn jacket, which he left in the emergency room at Bellevue Hospital. It was beyond the talents of even the best tailor. Between shuffling from the hospital to the police station and the repeated interviews with investigators and detectives about the incident, he had forgotten about it until now.

"No, sir. I am fine. Just a little headache. I'm sorry, can you repeat the question again?"

"Wasn't a question, Joe. It was a statement. I got a call from the FBI late this afternoon. They are coming over to the office tomorrow and want to meet with you and Ken. Wouldn't say what it was about, but they made clear they wanted use of a private conference room. You have any idea why they are coming to speak with you?"

"I can only assume it is to ask more questions about the attack."

"Yes, I assumed that. You let me know after the meeting, Joe, if there is anything that this firm may need to be concerned about. I alerted the chair of the criminal law department that he should be ready to assist you, if needed."

Joe swallowed and realized that things could really begin to spin out of control. "Don't think that will be needed, sir, but much appreciated. I'll report back after the meeting. What time did you say they are coming here?"

"Ten. Be ready. Be smart. Alright. Why don't you head home early and get some rest. A little too much excitement for one day, as far as I can see." With that, McDonald reached for his phone, which signaled that the meeting was over. Joe got up from the guest chair and headed back to his room. As soon as he entered his office, the door shut soundly behind him. Just then, he was suddenly grabbed from behind in a bear hug. Dalia kissed his cheeks and then professed in a stern voice, "Do that again, Joe, and I will personally kill you."

"How many people can a guy have trying to kill him in one day?" he responded, and then turned and kissed her full on the lips, holding the back of her head with his bandaged arm. The dark ponytail slipped between his fingers.

As she wiped the tears from under her eyes, Dalia quietly stated, "My mother was trying to reach you, Joe. The neighbor across the street was looking out her window last night and saw a man in dark car keeping an eye on my home. This is really getting scary."

Joe sat down at his desk. "We made someone real nervous with our investigation. We must be getting close."

Dalia opened the door to Joe's office and looked over her shoulder as she walked out. "Joe, you are not going to stop, are you?" He knew from her voice that the comment was part critical, and part concession that she knew he would not change. He felt a pang of guilt. Their deepening relationship made clear that he had a responsibility to keep her safe. *But the bad guy is now dead, Joe thought to himself. How many bad guys could there be?*

The phone rang. It was Ken. He asked softly if Joe was aware of the upcoming visit from the FBI. Joe responded that McDonald had just mentioned it. They were to be interviewed tomorrow morning at ten.

"You think they know, Joe?" the Captain said.

"No idea, Ken. But Dalia may be right. This whole thing is getting out of hand."

"Yeah. Well, I can't carry a flare gun on me everywhere we go. In fact, you now owe me a flare gun. The police confiscated it during their investigation."

That got a chuckle out of Joe. "I didn't think orange was your color in any event. Try next time to get one in mauve."

"Yeah, right." Ken hung up.

Joe dialed the phone, and a minute later, he was talking to Mike Graham. He summarized what had happened and commented that the attack was proof that his investigation must be making progress.

"Joe, the company never intended to put you or any of your team in any danger. If you feel this is beyond you, then bail. We can talk to a professional investigation team. However, I must admit that you have made more progress than anyone else. In fact, I have received calls from MI5 asking about how your investigation is proceeding. Seems they are keeping an eye on you, as well."

"Wish they were standing behind me this morning."

"I suspect they were not that far away, Joe. Keep me posted. What's your next move if you go forward with the case?"

"I think it's time we visited Mr. Hong in Seoul. Got a few questions for him. He is involved in the Pilot Fish, I know it. He may not be running it, but he is still in it, waist deep."

"I suspect you are right, but he is a powerful man. You have to be very careful with what you say. I don't want him filing lawsuits against the London marine insurance market because he feels he has been slandered. We have contacted his office and advised that we are performing a routine investigation about the collision with the *Crazy Horse*. Since it was his ship that was involved, he understands that we need to speak directly with him. Hong has agreed to give a few minutes and has offered to cooperate. We told his office that the investigator would be calling to make an appointment. We didn't give your name, but strangely, his office responded that they would do what they could for the American lawyer. We never said it was an American law firm handling the investigation. So, add that to your list of suspicious moments."

There was a pause, and then Nick commented in a fatherly tone, "And Joe, be careful. We want you around to work on other cases." He then hung up.

Chapter 17

Joe got up from his desk and walked down the hall to Captain Ken's office. He closed the door and summarized the call with London. They then began to sketch out on a legal pad what had to be done in Korea, and what needed to be said to Mr. Hong.

Chapter 18
Seoul

Hong Shipping had offices on the thirty-eighth floor with spectacular views of the harbor in Seoul. The top floor of the same modern building housed an excellent steak restaurant called Kogi, famous for its Korean barbecue. The view from the floor-to-ceiling windows were magnificent. The ancient city, with its curved roofs, Buddhist temples, and palaces, sprawled out for miles below them. Ships could be seen cutting trails of pearl-white wakes as they plied the dark-blue Han River which twisted through the city district. The service at Kogi was top notch, which was to be expected at a member's-only establishment. Dozens of very pretty and young women dressed in tight skirts, white silk blouses, and high heels, with perfectly coiffured hair, served high-powered executive men sitting at tables under low lighting. The walls were covered with rich dark slate and river stone. A waterfall flowed down one wall, creating peaceful background noise and making it a bit more difficult to hear the hushed private conversations at the tables. Strategically-placed topiary insured that the tables also enjoyed visual privacy as well.

A stunning hostess bent slowly over a bald and portly man at one table dressed in a very expensive suit that tried to disguise his lack of shape. She slowly poured from a bottle of thirty-year-old Macallan whiskey into his fist-sized crystal glass. She intentionally allowed a couple of wisps of her jet-black hair to lightly fall across the top of his bare head. He smiled as he looked up at her with his stained teeth, obviously enjoying the attention. The waitress knew that the two men at the table were discussing something very important and that her presence was to be limited. Having asked in a sweet voice if he was satisfied with the whiskey, Mr. Hong simply replied that it was alright. The lascivious look in his deep-set eyes had disappeared. He was obviously thinking of something other than the hostess. She excused herself, still bowing, and quietly moved away.

"So, tell me. What happened this time?" He looked up at the thin man sitting across from him. He was new; a replacement for the shadow who was always sneaking into his office or gardens. Apparently, the mystery man was now dead. Hong had no idea where the little dictator found these irritating rats that acted as intermediaries, but he was getting annoyed at their lack of success for all their touted skills.

"Our sources indicate that the operative was killed. Shot in the subway station in New York."

"Who shot him? The police?" Hong took another sip of the single malt. At least something was perfect.

"We don't think so. It appears Barrett's associate, the man they call Captain Ken, shot him with a flare gun."

Hong tried to digest the information, which was now interfering with his enjoyment of the fine scotch. *Ridiculous*, he thought. The Americans were taunting him. They could use plastic flare guns and take down the most highly-trained Hwarang, the Korean equivalent of a Japanese samurai warrior. This was really becoming a disaster. He needed to break his relationship with the devil from the North.

Hong started to lift his glass for another sip and realized his stomach really was bothering him. "What does your boss plan to do now?" asked Hong softly.

"There are many options. We have our eye on his girlfriend and her family."

The executive burped, putting his hand over his stomach. "What can that possibly achieve? Mr. Barrett must suspect by now that he is under observation and that efforts are being made to kill him and those close to him. He must have talked at the police station. It won't take long for the American government to figure out something is going on with those special submarines you built, and that it involves North Korea. I think we should stop everything we are doing…" Hong paused as he looked into the hardened eyes of his guest, and finally added "…and wait until this blows over."

The thin man twisted in his seat so that he could lean over the table in the direction of the old man. He looked up slowly and said in an icy tone, "You mean that your concern is that the American government may find out about your involvement, don't you?" He then leaned back, and with a hint of a snarl said, "Our sources in the New York police say there was neither any mention of the submarine by Mr. Barrett, nor the incident in Italy. There was also no mention of Korea, nor of your company. They blamed the incident on an unknown crazy man. So, you are safe, for now."

Hong could feel his bloated stomach protesting again. How stupid could they be to believe that information?

"Well, I do not feel safe. Mr. Barrett is coming to Seoul to see me about the collision and the submarine. I am sure we will discover that he knows a lot more than your sources in the police department. Frankly, I am taking a lot more risk than I bargained for with your boss. We need to start talking about how this relationship should come to an end."

The guest simply chuckled, and then covered his mouth with a napkin. "End? You must be very foolish, old man, to think that our respected chairman is going to end the relationship with your company. No, he has invested too much time and money. He is on a schedule and there is a deadline for his fireball. Any end to your relationship would probably come with a funeral. You will continue to perform as agreed, and I will omit mention of this comment in my report."

"I see, I have no choice. But your people have failed time and again. All I ask is that you keep my name out of this." He swigged the last drops of the whiskey down this throat, enjoying the warmth it carried with it.

"Why? Someday soon, my chairman will be giving orders from a building just down the street from your office. You will be famous and probably rewarded. The Hong name will be known around the world as bringing the Korean peninsula back together under one rule. What more could you possibly want?"

Hong could not hold back the belch, which was heard even by the young waitress who had approached with the bottle of Macallan on a velvet platter. He lifted his fat hand in the air and abruptly signaled her to take it away. There was no point in wasting such a fine drink on a calamity.

Chapter 19
New York

Tim neatly stacked some documents on the polished conference room table knowing that Joe Barrett would want to have some materials about the Pilot Fish available if the FBI asked really pointed questions. No one was certain how much they knew, and while the documents might be legally protected under the attorney-client or the attorney work-product privileges, Joe had already discussed with London that the client should be prepared to let Joe turn over some of the material if the FBI made a lot of noise. Better to volunteer a few selected documents then being served with subpoenas to turn over everything.

A few minutes later, Joe and Ken walked into the conference room carrying cups of coffee and talking in hushed tones. Joe looked briefly over at Dalia, who was putting out mats and legal pads around the table. There was no sign of nervousness. He suspected she was relieved that law enforcement was finally getting involved. Dalia did not doubt Joe's ability for a minute, but the case was no longer about practicing law.

An announcement over the speakerphone advised that three people were in the lobby waiting to see Mr. Barrett. Joe instructed that they be escorted immediately to the conference room. He then picked out a seat and sat down at the center of the long table. He had learned long ago that sitting at the end of the table just isolated the host and alienated the guests. Better to sit in the center of the table.

Chapter 19

The door to the conference room opened, and Joe's draw dropped.

Captain Ken looked over at the guests and was equally stunned. Leading a party of two men, who were obviously FBI agents in dark blue suits with dark ties and white shirts, was the distinctive short, cropped, red hair and freckled face of Yeoman Fox. She was dressed elegantly in a well-tailored skirt and jacket with a creamed colored ruffled blouse. A gold stickpin was fastened to her lapel. The Navy hat, insignia, and gold braid were missing. Her pursed lips finally gave way to a broad smile. She laid her leather briefcase gently on the table and immediately held out her hand to greet both Joe and Ken with a formal handshake. The look on Captain Ken's face was absolute amazement and confusion. He stiffly shook the yeoman's hand, not knowing what to say. He stared into her face in search of some message. All he saw was the twinkle of her light blue eyes. Ken awkwardly released her and invited the yeoman to take a seat.

"I know, you were not expecting me," she coyly commented.

"That is an understatement even by British standards," Joe responded with a cheerful voice.

"Yes, well, the fact is that I am on loan to MI5 in respect to our favorite subject. They are cooperating with your FBI on the investigation, and it was felt I knew more about the subject than anyone else. Well, perhaps with the exception of you two," looking at Joe and Ken. "Your efforts and achievements have been closely scrutinized on both sides of the pond."

"Huh?" was all that Joe could get out. Sensing the uncomfortable moment, Dalia immediately stepped next to Joe and said, "Perhaps we should all introduce ourselves. I am Dalia Pucci, a paralegal at the firm, and this is Tim Murphy, an associate. I gather you have already met Joe Barrett and Ken Libby." The last sentence was said with enough of an edge to it that Joe looked up, trying to remember what he had told Dalia about Ms. Fox. Not much, he realized.

"Dalia, it is really wonderful to meet you. Joe talked so much about you when he was in England. And I must admit that we were very impressed by your stealth getting into Professor Gehlardi's office in Genoa."

"You know about that?" Dalia stammered.

"Actually, we know quite a bit about what you have all been doing. That is why I am here. We need to discuss what has to be done next."

The red-head British officer stopped for a moment and added, "By the way, let me introduce you to Special Agents Lee and Park. They have been assigned by your government to assist on this matter. There are others in Washington who are also working on this project, but these two men are critical to the future operation."

"What future operation are you referring to?" asked Joe.

Fox sat across the table from Joe and looked him in the eye. "Before we get to that, I need to know what you believe you have discovered so far."

Joe shifted uncomfortably in his chair and then picked up a pencil. He remained silent for a moment, apparently organizing thoughts in his head.

"Best as we can determine, the Pilot Fish was probably built in a secret Chinese military yard, but the very advanced engines on board were designed in Italy for a company that has ties with North Korea. The vessel, and we think there is more than one, was intended for delivery to North Korea. Payment for the vessel was probably made by North Korea through laundered money made from the sale of Chinese cocaine and the delivery of North Korean coal to China. The sub was probably sneaked out of China attached underneath a series of ships operated by a subsidiary of Hong Lines involved in the carriage of coal to China.

Chapter 19

"We know all of this from the inspection of the Pilot Fish that was found after the collision. It was used to carry drugs and return with cash; but the vessel is much larger than needed to carry drugs. We think the North Koreans are planning on sneaking one or more of these subs into U.S. ports. Which ones we don't know, but Hong Lines only services the ports of Savannah, and New York on the East Coast. On the West Coast, they call at Los Angeles and Seattle. We doubt the ships were intended to carry troops or passengers. The accommodation for humans was limited to maybe two people – the pilots. It was most likely that the submarine or submarines are going to be used to bring something more deadly, like weapons or a bomb, into the U.S. Whatever it is, the North Koreans are rattled by our investigation and are willing to kill. And finally, we think that Hong Lines is involved because they have secretly been having severe money problems. We suspect they are getting some cash infusion from the operation."

Joe stopped and opened a bottle of water. He took a long sip. Everyone around the table remained silent and focused on Joe.

"The big problem," Barrett resumed, "is that those subs are invisible to most technology today. They are nearly invisible to sonar and radar, they are fast and silent, and they can remain underwater for long periods of time." He paused again, "We think the answers to what North Korea plans to eventually transport in the subs lie with Hong Lines. The shipowner has been involved from the beginning. Hong knows what the plan is."

The two FBI agents immediately began whispering to each other. One picked up his cell phone and left the conference room. Joe looked quizzically at Fox. She finally spoke.

"Mr. Barrett, I am impressed. It took a lot of people in both Washington and London to come to most of those conclusions as well."

Captain Ken finally spoke up. "Ms. Fox, what do you believe the subs are intended to carry and where they are going to go?"

"We are not sure, Mr. Libby, but our political analysts fear that it may be an effort by the North Koreans to bring the atom bombs they have developed to the shores of the United States and some other countries. We think North Korea is having problems solving the technical issues needed to get their ICBM missiles to survive re-entry into the atmosphere. The Pilot Fish provides an easy and undetectable way to achieve their threats."

Ken looked across the table. "You mean while everyone is looking up in the sky for an attack by the North Koreans, the North Koreans are invading underwater. Got to admit, it's brilliant."

"My thought as well. And if they are able to explode a bomb in the U.S. from beneath one of your harbors, no one will know for certain who did it."

Dalia finally sat and talked very slowly. "I still don't understand. You said you came here in respect to what 'we' need to do in future operations. What future operations? And why should they involve us? Isn't this now in the hands of the army or special forces?" The worried look on her face was obvious. Her eyes glistened. She instinctively wiped away a tear that appeared on her cheek. "Joe was almost killed this week. I don't see what more we can do."

Yeoman Fox answered quickly in a sharp, professional voice. "We know what happened in the subway. Yes, he was almost killed. But right now, if the North Koreans succeed in secretly bringing a nuclear weapon into the U.S., there will be a lot more lives at stake. Maybe even you and your family. Right now, Joe and Captain Ken have a big advantage over our governments. Mr. Hong has agreed to meet with them and discuss the situation because he needs the insurance money on the loss of his ship. He is not going to meet with the U.S. or British government."

"But Hong is not stupid. He is not going to admit to Joe that he plans on letting the subs carry bombs to the U.S.," Dalia protested.

"You are correct, Dalia. But with the help of Mr. Lee and Mr. Park, we hope that Joe will be able to leave some bugs in Hong's office that will let us listen to his future conversations and hack into his computer. Hopefully, we will learn enough details to stop the operation."

Joe now spoke up, realizing how serious the problem was from Dalia's perspective. "Why can't the South Korean government arrest him, or at least do the bugging?"

"It would be nice, indeed, if South Korea would get involved. But they are resisting our pleas because Hong Lines is a major company and an old family with significant political ties. They are equally concerned that, if we are right, it will create a huge embarrassment for South Korea. What we intend to do is illegal under Korean law, but we suspect their government is going to turn a blind-eye knowing the high stakes involved."

Joe and Ken looked at each other. It was obvious that there were no other solutions. "Alright, we will help, but you have to promise us that I won't be facing another samurai with a sharp sword on the street."

For the first time, Park spoke up. "Actually, they are called Hwarang in Korea, not samurai. That is Japanese. But you are correct, Mr. Barrett, they are just as deadly. I can assure you that we will be only steps away at all times. We will have your back. Leaving the bugs in Mr. Hong's office will only take seconds. We will train you and Mr. Libby on how to do it. We will also equip you with communication equipment that will keep us in constant contact with both of you."

"OK," said Joe, "where do we begin?"

Dalia quietly got up from her chair and left the room without saying a word.

Chapter 20
Pacific Ocean

The young submarine pilot sat absolutely motionless, except for his right hand, which deftly maneuvered a joystick mounted at the end of the armrest on the comfortable leather chair in which he was seated. His eyes were riveted on the large screen overhead. The display was a wide-angle video of dark-colored steel plates taken underwater. Barnacles, bubbles, scrapes, and pitted paint could be seen along the long hull. The entire image appeared a strange green color because of the "night vision" technology used; in fact, it was actually mid-afternoon in the Yellow Sea near Busan. However, because the sub was underneath the huge container vessel, the shadow overhead caused the water around them to turn almost black. The container ship, which was named *Wild Pony*, was one of the largest and newest ships in Hong Lines' fleet. It carried nearly 14,000 containers, and was assigned to the trade between China, Korea, and the East Coast of the United States. The ship was only a little more than half full, for reasons that were not at all clear to its captain, given that Christmas deliveries to the United States were already in full swing. The result was that she only drew about twenty-five feet in draft, rather than her normal thirty-eight feet. That was coincidentally good for the submersible because she would be able to remain latched onto the bottom of the cargo ship as it went through the Panama Canal and into New York harbor where the maximum depth was only forty feet.

With a slight twist of the joystick and the pressing of a red button on its tip, the sub engaged its electromagnets and securely attached itself to the underside of the *Wild Pony* with hardly a sound. If the container ship's crew heard anything, they would assume it was some debris that hit the hull and washed away.

When he was certain that they were locked in place, the pilot lay back in his thick seat and smiled. He turned to the co-pilot and instructed him to shut down the engines and send a message that the vessel was locked in place and ready to begin its long voyage. A slight humming through the ship went dead when the co-pilot flipped some switches. It was eerily quiet and the red lights used in the cabin only contributed to the surreal atmosphere. The pilot shifted the position of his armchair and stood up to stretch. It had been more than fifteen hours since they left the port of Nampo on the western side of North Korea after loading their special cargo. They were now at a point off the entrance to the Han River, where cargo ships were required to drop their harbor pilots to waiting tug boats. It was simply a matter of staying underwater until the *Wild Pony* came out of Busan. She was right on schedule.

The lean pilot, who had graduated at the top of his military nautical class only five years earlier, turned to get a fresh bottle of water from the galley. The moment he rotated, he involuntarily froze for a moment as he faced two large caskets that sat only ten feet from the back of his chair. The boxes were made of highly polished steel. Each one was at least twelve feet long and about six feet wide. They were also about five feet high. The boxes sat directly on top of the bay doors built into the deck that opened to the sea below. The metallic crates had been secured with several straps and clamps at the deck level to ensure that they did not accidentally shift while the sub moved underwater.

Chapter 20

Jin was very proud of the fact that he and his co-pilot, Bae, had been selected for the mission. But the sad and inescapable fact was that it would most likely end in their suicide. For Jin, that was not a problem as he was single and his parents were dead. He was devoted to his job and his struggling country. But Bae's young wife had just given birth to their first child, a girl. She and the baby lived with his parents and his sisters in a small apartment near the naval base. Bae kept a small black and white photo of his entire family taped on his armrest, near the secondary joystick. He had been quiet the entire voyage, although he had performed all of his tasks admirably.

"I wish they had erected a wall or a curtain so we don't have to stare at these tombstones every time we get up," Jin said.

"I don't think a cotton curtain or even a metal wall would do us much good if they exploded," Bae responded in a somber voice.

Jin was not certain how to reply to the gallows humor and decided to focus on getting the bottle of water. The small fridge held about a dozen bottles and struggled to keep them chilled. He opened the plastic top and took a long swig of cool water. Wiping his mouth with the back of his hand, he replaced the cap and looked at the stacks of tins on the shelves. "Well, my good friend, you have a choice of tuna or salmon for dinner. You can have it any way you like, so long as we eat it straight out of the can."

Bae said nothing, and continued working on the electronic navigational charts. Bae's job was to add just enough thrust from the submarine during the crossing of the Pacific so that the handling of the cargo ship was not impacted by the drag of the sub leeched to mother vessel. Otherwise, some seaman on the *Wild Pony* might get curious about why their ship was pulling to one side and going slower than expected. With only one pilot, this task could not be done.

Jin looked over and realized it was best not to antagonize his childhood friend. He walked aft to the bunk bed, and, with some agility, slipped into the bottom one. He covered himself with a wool blanket to ward off the constant chill and damp air inside the sub. Putting his hands behind his head, Jin quickly calculated that, within twenty-five days, they should be in New York. Then, the fun would start. Then, they would be dead.

Chapter 21
New York

"Let's go have a drink at Maggie's, just the two of us, like old times," Joe offered while craning his neck around the opening to Dalia's paralegal station. He put on a wide grin, but knew that was not going to help. "Come on!"

At first, Dalia kept flipping through some pages from a tall stack of paper on her desk. She then looked up with a cold stare, and without saying a word, stood up and grabbed her coat from the hook on the wall. "OK, let's go get that drink." She mechanically followed him down the hallway and into the elevator lobby.

In the elevator, they just stared at the electronic monitor over the floor buttons that gave news briefs. One of the clips was about the Seventh Fleet performing exercises off the coast of Korea in coordination with Japan and Australia. The obligatory photos of warplanes taking off from an aircraft carrier's deck with smoke and belching fire were included. As they entered the worn shellacked doors of Maggie's, the hostess was on the phone but looked up and gave a cheerful smile to Dalia and pointed them to some empty seating in the back. The bar had been around for over a hundred years and was popular with the business people in the area. Several employees greeted Dalia in the narrow hallway as she put on a forced smile and said "hi" to each of them. Dalia had worked behind the bar at Maggie's for over a year before being recruited by Joe to help him as a translator on a case involving two Syrian children who arrived in the United States as stowaways. She had done such a remarkable job that his firm offered her a position as a paralegal. Now, she wasn't so sure that she had made the right decision. Perhaps she had done some good and brought happiness to the lives of those children, but Joe's job carried a lot of risks that you did not encounter as a bartender. Drunks and broken glasses were not in the same category as swords and bombs. Joe ordered them both a glass of draft beer and they discussed preparation for Thanksgiving, which was less than a couple of weeks away. At a quiet moment in the conversation, Joe reached out and held both her hands. He did not say anything for a moment and then spoke directly to her as he leaned forward.

"You know that I love you very much, and I love your son and your mother. I would not want to see anyone get hurt – especially you. But I can't hide from what is happening. What I am doing is to protect everyone I love from what could be a real disaster."

He studied her face. "You know what I remember most about you in this place?" He scanned the room in both directions. "It was the anger in your breath and the fire in your eyes when, a year ago, you looked up at that crappy old television set over the bar and saw the picture of Mohammed al-Aishen on the news. You cursed and muttered in Arabic, and when I asked what you were saying, you called him a bastard and said he had to be eliminated. You said that people like him did not deserve to live. Well, you and I got rid of al-Aishen but now there is another one, just as dangerous, and a lot more deadly. I am not a hero, but if I can help stop the threat, then I know my loved ones are a little bit safer." He lifted her hands up off the table and looked into her eyes, which were now both very wet.

"I can't believe you brought me here," she sniffled, "Just so you could use that incident against me. That is so unfair!" She finally chuckled, wiped her eyes dry while holding back the urge to start sobbing, and held on tight to his hands. "I know you love me and my family, and I know I can't stop you. I am only asking that we share our lives together, for a very long time. Joe, I am going to say this just once: don't get yourself killed. That is all that I ask."

She leaned over the small table and kissed him fully on the lips. Wiping away the last of the tears, she said finally, "You take a girl out on a date and all you buy her is one beer? I think you should at least offer a cheeseburger. I hear they do a pretty good job here with burgers."

Joe smiled and looked for the waitress. His only concern now was whether he could keep his promise of staying alive.

Chapter 22
Manhattan

The white stucco façade of Sam's Place on 39th Street wasn't difficult to find, but getting a table in the back was remarkable. The small, family–style restaurant only accommodated a dozen tables, and on most nights it was packed with locals and visitors from a nearby hotel. The owner, Max, dressed in a black suit, smiled as he served a tasting sample of Castell'in Villa Chianti Classic Riserva into a broad mouth goblet for the handsome man and young lady. Her copper-red hair and beautiful blue eyes particularly impressed him, not to mention the soft English accent.

Placing his hand gently on the shoulder of the bearded man, a touch Max used with all his long-time customers, he waited till the ruby-red liquor had been sipped.

"*Fa bene?*" the owner asked.

Ken looked up and responded, "You picked a good one tonight, Max. I don't know who supplies your wines, but he has good taste."

"Kenny, you know I pick all the wines! How long have you been coming here? Twenty years. Have you ever had a bad wine? Now, let me give some time for you and the lovely lady to study the menu. But, as you know, I will make whatever you want." Max moved to the far table where another couple was just seated.

"So, how long have you been coming here? Or is Max your cousin?" Yeoman Fox smiled mischievously, and then lifted the velvet wine and clinked glasses before taking a long, deliberate sip. "My, that is good." Looking around the tiny room, which had oddly matched paintings hanging on the wall, she looked at Ken, and commented, "I never would have found this restaurant."

"It's not in the travel books. Max does enough business without advertising. He even has customers who live in the neighborhood and eat here every day rather than try to cook in their tiny kitchens. "

Ken put his glass down, picked up the menu, observed her coy smile and twinkling eyes, and put the menu back on the table.

"So, Ms. Deborah Fox, are you going to let me in on when you became Ms. Jamie Bond?"

She briefly laughed, and then straightened up. "I am not a spy, at least not yet. Just a naval officer, like you were once. But intelligence thought I could help on this case, and I agreed to give it a try." There was a pause, and then another mischievous glance. "Well, of course, once they told me that I would have to go to New York, there was an incentive."

"Do they know about us? I mean your employers?"

"Probably. They are pretty good at keeping tabs. There might even be a recorder taped to the bottom of this table." Another hint of a wicked smile flashed across her face. "But I am not violating any rules. And I do want to pick up where we left off in London. I have really enjoyed your emails and phone calls since then, but I think we need some human contact. By the way, as long as we are revealing secrets, does Mr. Barrett know?

Captain. Ken nervously picked up the menu, which he already knew by heart. "No, I haven't said a word to him. You asked me before I got on the helicopter in Southampton to keep it quiet. I have."

"Well, I think you now have to tell him the truth. We can't go on with any trust issues. Frankly, I was not certain he would agree to this job given his relationship with Ms. Pucci.

There is certainly some risk of danger. I will do what I can to give you fellows the best protection, but you know there can't be any guarantees."

"Where will you be?"

"At the British Embassy in Seoul. A team that will be providing surveillance of your every move. The FBI will be working with us. A lot of good people are involved in this project."

Max slowly walked over to their table once more, noting that their private conversation seemed to have hit an intermission. He went through a list of suggested dishes with anecdotes about some of his more famous customers. He poured each of them more wine, and then quietly left their table.

"So, I guess MI5 has a dossier of all my emails to you over the past month?" he queried in a serious tone.

"You forgot about all the phone conversations they taped. Ken, I don't think they care about our relationship. What they care about is success on the job. I think we can do this. We are monitoring Hong's entire fleet. They have made a list of every person coming in and out of his offices. Some of his phones are tapped. He is followed outside of his office. One of our operatives served his table at a private steak restaurant in Seoul a couple of days ago. Something is up. The man who he was with could not be identified, but he was overhead to say that there was a deadline by the 'chairman.' The chairman was not identified, but I think we all know who he was referring to. They would not allow Hong to delay their schedule." Fox looked around to make sure no one was watching, and then whispered, "And there was a reference to a 'fireball.' That was all she could make out from reading lips and hearing bits of words."

"Could be nothing. Just corporate stuff."

Fox picked up her menu and looked at Ken over her reading glasses. "But what if it isn't? What if fireball means just what we think it means? That's why we need you and Joe."

"Fireball?" he said glumly. "Let's stay away from the spicy stuff tonight."

She quickly responded, "I was saving it for dessert," as Max approached their table for the third time with his pad in hand.

CHAPTER 23
KOREA

"Coffee or tea, sir?" asked the attractive young stewardess dressed in the standard red and khaki colors of Asiana Airlines.

Joe opened one blue eye and stared at the hostess. She smiled and held two pots in front of her. He rubbed his unshaven cheeks, tussled his hair, and straightened up in the narrow seat. "Coffee, please…" he mumbled. On his left, Captain Ken had also just awoken. He was trying to stretch and do a few yoga moves after ten hours in the air. The two had eaten very little and spent most of the flight reading papers and talking in hushed tones. They both looked exhausted.

Joe signaled to the stewardess that Captain Ken wanted a cup as well.

"Will Ms. Fox be joining us in the cab from the airport to the hotel?" Joe said this last part with just enough of a grin on his face to make it clear he was having fun. In fact, Yeoman Fox was sitting eight aisles behind them with her two FBI friends.

Ken didn't pause to reply. "No, she is heading off to the embassy. We take a taxi straight to the hotel. I don't think we will be seeing much of her in Seoul. Might send the wrong message."

"To the North Koreans or to the British government?" Joe chuckled.

Ken looked away, refusing to blush. "Perhaps both," he responded. "Sorry I didn't tell you more about her, but as I have now stated a half-dozen times, she ordered me not to mention our relationship when we got off the helicopter in London."

"Ken, I'm just pulling your leg. Not to worry. I really like her, and I think she would be good for you. Enough said. Let's go over some of the questions we want to press Mr. Hong with when we have our meeting tomorrow."

Joe and Ken breezed through Immigration and Customs at the Inchon International Airport. Heading through the immense white marble lobby of the modern airport toward the taxi stand, they were approached by a man in a dark suit, hat, and white gloves carrying a sign with both their names written on it. He stopped in front of them, looking at his phone, probably trying to match them with some photo he had been given.

"Mr. Barrett, Mr. Libby, I am Kyu Park, your driver. Mr. Hong asked that I pick you up and drive you directly to your hotel as a courtesy given your long flight. Please, let me take your luggage." His English was heavily accented but the tone in his voice was very composed.

"No, thank you, but...." Joe was cut off by Ken, who finished the sentence, "No, but we can carry our own luggage. It was very nice of Mr. Hong to offer us his car. We will follow you."

Joe gave Captain Ken a disapproving look. He was not in favor of taking any rides offered by Hong Lines. Ken simply shifted his eyes to the far right three times before Joe got the idea to look over to their right. Ms. Fox was standing behind a railing about a hundred feet away, and while not looking at the two men, it was clear she was nodding her head up and down. Joe shrugged and picked up his bag to follow the man.

As they were about to go through the large revolving door to the street, Ken was suddenly knocked over by a passenger racing to get to the same door. The red-headed lady stopped and in a distinct British accent quickly apologized for the incident. Ken played a straight face, although the fall had, in fact, taken a little wind out of him. As he struggled to stand, she put her hand around his waist and helped him to his feet before straightening the collar on his jacket. Fox smiled, said again how sorry she was, and dashed through the door. Ken noticed that throughout all the theatrics, never once did she face the driver. As he straightened out his coat, he realized there was something in his peacoat pocket. Ken then pointed to his bag and asked the driver to carry it, as he held his back feigning some pain. Joe looked at Ken seeking some message about what had happened. All he saw was Ken's poker face.

The driver approached his car, a black, top-of-the line Genesis, which had the distinctive look of a Mercedes. It was empty and parked at the curb. Given the number of policemen chasing drivers away from the curbside, parking at the curb was an impressive – or an expensive – feat, thought Joe. The luggage was placed in the trunk and the two men sat in the back. Joe was impressed with the deep rich leather seats and the burl wood trim. A shelf with top label liquors in French crystal bottles was built into the back of the front seat. Apparently, Hong had actually sent his own car. The driver sent a quick text after starting the car. The huge 429-horsepower, V-8 engine made a soft, throaty sound. The driver turned and with a smile composed mostly of small, sharp teeth, commented, "I believe you are staying at the Intercontinental Hotel, am I correct?"

Joe's eyes hardened. "Yes, that is correct. I was not aware that we had told Mr. Hong where we would be staying in Seoul."

"Mr. Hong knows everything in Korea. He is very powerful man." The car moved forward effortlessly and headed for the highway.

"I am impressed that he has so much influence. How large is his office in Seoul?"

"Oh, the company has more than fifteen hundred people working in the office. Over thirty thousand around the world."

Joe decided to see if he could keep the driver talking. If he was indeed Hong's personal driver, he presumably overheard a lot of conversations in the back seat. "Does Mr. Hong have offices in other countries like, say, China?" Joe asked in a serious but innocent tone. "Yes, Mr. Hong's ships go to China. Many ships. Many offices. China is a good customer."

"Really? China is a big country. I thought they just sold goods to other countries. What does Hong bring to a place like China from Korea?"

"The driver smiled and replied, "All kinds of cargo. Containers from Samsung, LG, Hyundai, lots of big names."

Joe paused and then asked, "Oh, I thought it would have been loose cargo, like grain or coal?"

The driver did not hesitate, showing pride for his employer, "Oh yes, we ship rice and coal to China"

"But the coal comes from North Korea, right?" said Joe. "I don't think they ship coal from South Korea."

There was a moment of hesitation before the driver answered, suddenly with signs of faltering English, "We are in South Korea. We do not do business with North Korea. Mr. Hong does business all over world. Everywhere in world." After providing the inscrutable answer, the driver turned on the radio. Classical music drifted through the cabin. The chauffeur gave a toothy smile in the mirror and then focused on the dark road in front of them. Sunrise was still an hour away.

On the assumption that the car was bugged, Joe and Ken continued to talk about the weather and sports as the car rolled along. About twenty minutes later, as they passed a road sign, Captain Ken sat up and said to the driver, "Why are we heading south towards Daejon? Shouldn't we be taking the eastern road towards Seoul?" Joe looked at Ken and could see the concern on his face.

"Too much traffic on main road to Seoul. Faster if we take this route," was the reply from the smiling driver.

"I don't think so, Mr. Park. When I was a captain, I often took this drive from the airport to get back to my ship. The road to Seoul is a major highway. I suggest you turn around and head back to the highway to Seoul."

With a sneer, the chauffeur remarked, "I take you where Mr. Hong tells me to. I don't take instructions from you."

"Where are you taking us?" demanded Joe.

"Someplace where you stop asking questions." With that, he slowed the car down and pulled over to a stop. The road, which was fairly empty at such an early hour, had a service area off to its side. The driver put the automobile in park, and then reached with his right hand into his breast pocket and pulled out a small 9 mm pistol with almost lightning speed. As he began to turn his head to face the passengers in the back seat, he snarled, "Place your mobile phones on the front seat. Both of you. You won't need them where I am taking you." Suddenly, the strong accent was missing from his speech.

The problem with sitting in a left-side driver's seat, and trying to use a gun on those sitting behind you, is that your right forearm does not bend backward. You have to twist around to face those behind you. As the chauffeur bent his elbow forward to turn around, his gun briefly pointed at the dashboard. At the same moment, the driver could feel a cold steel barrel up against his right ear.

Ken cocked the pistol in his hand, without taking the barrel out of the driver's ear. "Now, why don't you just drop that gun on the seat next to you so that my partner can pick it up? Then, I want you to do the same with your cell phone. Very slow. Keep the left hand on top of the steering wheel. I assure you, I know how to shoot. Already shot one person this week. "

Joe looked at Ken quizzically. "Where the hell did you get a gun? We went through airport security." Ken looked over at Joe and winked. "A gift from my girlfriend. She left it in my pocket."

Joe shrugged and picked up the driver's pistol and his phone. At the same moment, a dark blue van drove up alongside their car and swerved to a stop directly in front of the Genesis so as to block it from further movement. Joe assumed Hong had sent a back-up to follow the driver. He wasn't prepared for a shoot-out. That only happened in the movies. Besides, they were trapped inside the car, and the two large men dressed in black fatigues that stepped out of the van were carrying automatic weapons.

"Don't worry, they're on our side," Ken commented as he rolled down his window and said to the first figure, "We have his pistol and phone." The driver's door was jerked open by the two men, who were obviously military. Although he tried to resist, the driver's arms were pinned behind him and quickly secured with plastic ties. Then his feet were tied. A bag was pulled over his head. They picked the driver up by his elbows and carried him to the van where he was pushed through the side door. The whole incident probably lasted less than a minute.

Yeoman Fox's red hair suddenly appeared through the driver's door as she smiled to the men in the back seat. "You can uncock your pistol now, Ken. I don't want anyone to get hurt." Ken laughed and handed the gun over to Yeoman Fox.

"I don't understand why you wanted us to get in the car in the first place? Didn't you suspect this was going to happen?" responded Joe, showing signs of some irritation.

"You are correct, Mr. Barrett. But until we saw the driver at the airport, we had no idea that Hong was trying to take action against the two of you at such an early stage. A bit surprising, actually, as we thought he would have waited until after the interview so as to first find out how much you knew about the Pilot Fish. Perhaps he thought he could get the same information from you beforehand, with some additional persuasion. In any event, we wanted to make sure the driver texted Hong that he had you in the car before we made any move."

Fox sat on the driver's seat facing them. "I am going to put Mr. Lee from the FBI in this car and have him drive you to the hotel. He looks a little bit like your chauffeur, and even more so once he borrows the driver's hat, gloves, and jacket. When you get out of the car, there will be witnesses that the driver dropped you off at the hotel. Hong won't know what happened to his driver. This should give you some leverage when you show up at his office tomorrow. If he asks about the driver, just say he dropped you off at the hotel and thank him for the courtesy. All Hong will know is that his driver failed to kidnap you, now he is missing and something has seriously gone wrong."

As she started to back away from the car door, Fox had a second thought and leaned back inside the car. "By the way, Mr. Barrett, that was an impressive bit of questioning about the coal from North Korea. I don't think Mr. Hong would have appreciated it at all. Probably better for the driver to be in our custody now. You gave us a bonus with the chauffeur. We have several new questions for him. We suspect, like you, that he has overheard a lot of Mr. Hong's conversations inside the car."

Joe stammered, "How did you know about my questions concerning the coal shipments?"

Fox leaned over the seat and quickly kissed Ken on the cheek. She pulled back his coat lapel. A gold-colored pin was secured on the underside of the collar. Fox had attached it when she collided with Ken at the airport. "Keep it," she said. "Might help you fellows stay out of trouble." Yeoman

Chapter 23

Fox smiled and headed back to the van. The moment she was inside the van, its lights came back on and it quickly accelerated back onto the highway.

A lean, athletically-built Korean man got into the van, tipped his hat, and introduced himself as Geoffrey. He started the engine and carefully shifted into forward. Now that, thought Joe, was a proper name for a chauffeur.

Chapter 24
Balboa

Jesus Garcia, Captain of the Port in Balboa, Panama, was staring out the large windows of his office onto the huge harbor. Ships were seemingly lined up to the horizon, waiting to go through the Miraflores locks to the Panama Canal. In fact, there were now two canals that transversed the Isthmus. A new canal, designed for the larger and more modern ships, was opened in 2017. It was helping reduce the backlog of traffic trying to cross from the Pacific to the Atlantic oceans. However, the fact was that the canal was more popular than ever, and with Christmas only two months away, the traffic through the canals was now reaching a peak as the retailers in the U.S. and in Europe stocked their stores in preparation for the holidays.

Garcia had retired from being a sea captain many years ago. In his fifties and fit, he found that being at sea for six months or more was lonely and boring. Work for a captain on a modern ship consisted of mostly filling out paperwork. In truth, there was very little glamor to the job. With international laws rapidly changing with the times, ship captains were now often the target of criminal laws. When governments couldn't find the shell company that managed a cargo ship, and there were serious issues involving oil spills or pollution, drugs, or poor treatment of the crew, it was the Master who often found himself in jail. Ships were even arrested by many legal regimes when something went wrong, and were not released until the owner showed up and posted very expensive security for the ship. Putting aside the changes in maritime laws, life at sea had also changed. Cargo ships could often be on such tight schedules that they went into and left the same port in less than a day. There was no longer time for seamen to go ashore and have a beer, or a woman. *Better to live on land, thought Garcia, than undertake the life of a ship's captain.*

"Captain, here is the log for the vessels going eastbound today through the canals. It looks like there are nearly two hundred."

"Yes, Ms. Negron. I can see them out my window. And there will be another two hundred tomorrow. Is there anything unusual on today's list that I should be aware of?"

The busty secretary with long black hair and black eyes quickly ran her finger down the list. "No, sir. Looks like there are four cruise ships, about twenty yachts, and fourteen tankers. Only one is carrying LNG. The rest appear to be mostly box ships."

"Tis the season, Ms. Negron. Have you started preparing for Christmas yet?" He spoke with a painful look on his face. "My wife tells me that we have the entire family coming for dinner."

"Yes, sir. My children are looking forward to it." Ms. Negron then gave a smile and noted, "By the way, all the documents seem to be in order today. Maybe that's my Christmas gift. Only thing I found curious was that one of the new Hong Lines ships is coming through today, but it's only half-loaded with cargo. Let me see. Here it is, the *Wild Pony*."

"Isn't she out in the harbor on the waiting line?" asked the port captain.

"Yes. Over there," pointing straight out the window towards the long cue of ships.

"Well, that is strange. We must have had four ships this week alone with Hong Lines, and each one was down to her marks in the water. Guess someone screwed up and failed to plan the loading of that ship, or they ran out of cargo in China? Hard to believe." The port captain picked up his binoculars and scanned the ships waiting in line. It was not hard to pick out the *Wild Pony* as the mass of red-colored bottom paint below her black water line was at least ten feet above the surface of the bay. The captain refocused his binoculars. More curious, he thought was the fact that the ship seemed to have a slight list to the port side. Most captains corrected that problem with water pumped from the sea into ballast tanks at the bottom of the ship so as to maintain stability. *Kind of sloppy,* he thought. Jesus picked up the VHF handset and called the ship, asking to speak with its captain. There was a lengthy wait while the call was transferred to the bridge.

"Hello? This is Captain Seo-Yen of vessel *Wild Pony*. Who am I speaking to?"

"Morning Captain. I am Captain Garcia, the port captain. I noticed from my office window that your vessel is listing to port. Am I correct? Not sure if you are aware of the condition."

There was a slight hesitation, and then the Master replied, "Ah, yes, that is correct. It is only five percent. We had some difficulties with our ballasting system as we came into the harbor this morning. Thank you for noting."

"Nothing serious I hope," replied the port captain. "Am I correct your vessel will be stable for the canal?"

"Yes, sir. No problems. We will correct when we arrive at Colon." The captain of the *Wild Pony* seemed a bit nervous on the radio.

Jesus was about to ring off the call when he smiled and said into the handset, "By the way, did they run out of Christmas toys in China? You are the only ship not fully loaded this whole week."

The VHF clicked a couple of times and then Captain Seo-Yen responded, "I am not certain as to why the ship is not full. I asked myself same question. The company loads the ships; I just steer it where they want." This was followed by an awkward, forced laugh.

"OK, Captain. Wish you calm seas ahead. Please proceed in line." The Port Captain returned the headset to its bracket and then picked up the binoculars again. Something was not right. Thirty years at sea told him he was missing something. He picked up the phone and called the Panamanian Coast Guard to keep their eye on the *Wild Pony.* "By the way," he said as he ended the call, "you might as well let the American Coast Guard know as well. I understand the ship is headed to Savannah."

Chapter 25
Panama Canal

The thunderous thrashing sound of the two giant propellers continuously turning on the cargo ship above them had gone silent several hours ago. It was a welcome silence to Jian and Bae after more than ten days of crossing the Pacific Ocean. Cans of tuna and salmon lay open in a cardboard box, allowing the atmosphere in the sub to be tainted with a fish smell even after the machinery scrubbed the atmosphere. The two men played another round of Godori, a Korean card game, while sitting on the deck. Jian was obviously pleased with having won colorful bonus cards from the hwatu deck. Bae did not respond, and continued to be moody and quiet. What little he said during the voyage was either about technical matters or how he worried how his family was doing without him. Otherwise, he stared at the monitor screen or at the photo of his family.

"I guess we are about to enter the Panama Canal," Jian announced. "By tonight, we should be on the Atlantic side. In four or five more days, we will be arriving at the port of Savannah." He slapped another card down and called "Matgo," the winning hand. "I wonder what Savannah looks like. It is probably decadent, with McDonald's and Kentucky Fried Chicken stores everywhere."

Bae stood up and moved his back, which was aching from sitting on the floor. "Frankly, I would not mind some chicken now, or even, what do they call it, a hamburger. I am tired of all this canned fish. Given that we are risking our lives, I think the Ministry could have given us some proper food for this trip. Some fruit, some turkey, and at least some rice cakes. We are no better than prisoners."

"My dear friend, don't say that. Out of the hundreds of applicants, only six of us were chosen for this program. One has already died. What we are doing is an honor for the Chairman."

"The Chairman is not sitting in a room with two atomic bombs next to his head. He is not the one who is going to drop the bomb in the harbors and hope that it does not go off under his ass. He is not the one that is going to be blown up by the American Navy when they find out what we have done. You and I know this is a suicide mission. I am only here for the sake of my family. Hopefully, they will get the extra rations of food and clothing that the Admiral promised when I was ordered to go. But it will not be the Chairman that I am thinking of when this boat is blown out of the water." Bae turned and sat down in the co-pilot seat so that he could once more look at the photo of his family.

Jian realized it was better to say nothing. He walked over to the pilot station and took the time to review all of the readings on the monitor and on the panel. He tapped on one of the dials, and with a worried expression, looked over at Bae. "You know, we are still not at a correct angle, The ship above us is listing four or five degrees. What do you think is wrong with our ballast compensation?"

Bae looked up at Jian and quietly remarked, "You remember that they insisted we attach ourselves as close as possible to the center of the bottom of the cargo ship? Well, we did. Now our sub's ballast tanks are not as effective as if we had attached ourselves nearer the water line of one side or the other. That was the old procedure, until special submarine number one was crushed in a collision in the English Channel last month. I have adjusted our tanks as much as possible to correct the angle, but the tanks cannot make up for the extra weight and drag we are putting on the *Wild Pony*. I only hope the ship's captain hasn't already noticed." After a moment, he added, "Maybe in the freshwater environment of the Canal, the list will not be as bad."

"I am more worried about being crushed under the ship when they release the water from each of the canal locks on the Atlantic side. Hopefully, our Navy has correctly calculated the cargo ship's draft and the free space underwater throughout the canal. Otherwise, we are going to look like one of those empty cans of tuna." He nodded over to the box where the tops of the cans of fish had been ripped open with a knife.

"I would still like a bite of chicken and rice," said Bae as he opened the computer and started running calculations one more time.

Chapter 26
Virginia

There was always a flurry of activity going on in the offices of the U.S. Coast Guard, Fifth District, on Crawford Street in downtown Portsmouth, Virginia. The District was responsible for the safety and security of the oceans, coastal areas, and marine transportation system in the Mid-Atlantic region, ranging from South Carolina to Maine, an area in excess of 150,000 square miles. It encompassed several major ports, the largest naval base in the world, and the nation's capital.

Master Chief Petty Officer Christine Milagros joined the Coast Guard in 1994 and quickly advanced through the ranks to become an operations specialist overseeing the chains of communications and information throughout the District, and with other Districts and governmental agencies. She was regarded as being very bright and driven, and had a memory for details. She ascended through the ranks with relative ease, making very few enemies along the way. Her natural smile disarmed many in the ranks, and her efforts to succeed caused her to put in long hours at the job.

From her desk, she looked down at the Elizabeth River, which led to the harbor in Hampton Roads. She was feeling a bit overwhelmed by the amount of paperwork that crossed her desk every day. The emails and faxes piled high on her desk were communications that had been pulled by her staff because they potentially required some sort of action. The decision on whether to take action or merely file the communications away as routine was ultimately her responsibility. If they had only given her a crystal ball when she accepted the job, it might have been more manageable. When she had previously attended the Sloan School of Management at MIT, no professor had provided any helpful hints on how to quickly and effectively pick the hidden needles out of haystacks. The process was unavoidably slow and elaborate.

In her hand, she held a faxed report from the Panamanian Coast Guard regarding what she initially thought was a silly and frivolous message. They had advised that a container ship, the *Wild Pony*, was listing slightly as it went through the Canal, and moreover, was not completely filled with cargo. She was about to toss the piece of paper when she noticed that her assistant, had scribbled a notation that the vessel was owned by "Hong Lines." She remembered a report of a collision in the English Channel a couple of months earlier that involved a Hong Lines vessel. She assumed the new message was totally unrelated to that situation, but recalled that the collision, for some reason, had triggered an investigation in Washington, D.C. The offices of the Coast Guard were asked to report upon anything unusual regarding ships operated by Hong Lines. Of course, no parameters were given as to what constituted "anything unusual," which was exactly why she remembered this tidbit of information.

The master chief petty officer called in her assistant, Roseann Burkhard, and asked her to take a seat.

"Rose, at first I thought this fax from the Canal about the *Wild Pony* was a joke, and I was just about to toss it in my trash can. But then I remembered that Hong Lines has been the subject of some kind of investigation in Washington. Not sure who is running it or why. Can you make some calls around and see who is handling the investigation? Maybe this fax is non-sense, or maybe it isn't. But I have this feeling in my stomach it shouldn't be tossed just yet. Meanwhile, let me talk to our base commander and see if he knows anything."

"Yes, Ma'am. I'll get to it right now." Her assistant went back to her desk and started working at her computer.

Christine picked up the phone and dialed the office of Captain Greg Sentori, who was the chief of staff for the Fifth District. He was a smart guy, a career cutterman with a dozen years of sea duty, and had previously worked as Chief of Response and Law Enforcement in Miami, Florida. When she heard the strong baritone voice of the captain at the other end of the phone, she requested permission to come by his office for five minutes. He responded to do it quickly as the rest of the day was tied up in meetings.

As the master chief petty officer entered the commander's room, she halted and waited patiently for him to get off the phone. Although the commander was not a stickler for formality in his office, he did require that one not speak until he spoke first. As Captain Sentori put down the phone, he methodically made a note in his desk book, then gently put his reading glasses down on the table and finally looked up at Christine.

"What's up? Not often you need to seek my help."

"Commander, I just received a fairly bizarre communication from the Panamanian Coast Guard regarding a container ship that just left Colon with a slight list and only half-filled with containers. They wanted us to be aware."

Greg chuckled and indicated to Christine to take a seat. "Now, we have to monitor seasonal sales and inclinometers, is that it?"

"Actually, sir, I was about to toss the fax as being ridiculous when I realized the ship they were referencing was one of the new Hong Line vessels, the *Wild Pony*. And she is reported as being headed for Savannah."

"Isn't that the Korean owner that was involved in the collision in the English Channel?" the captain asked.

"Yes, sir. That was Hong Lines. And I remember there was some investigation going on in Washington about the company afterward. Not sure what it was about, but I thought it best to check with you before I throw this out."

Captain Greg put his reading glasses back on and searched around his desk. He found a little black book and opened it. He immediately found the number he was looking for and began dialing. He looked over his shoulder at Christine and said, "Good work, Christine. What you don't know about that collision in the channel is that there was an advanced submarine that was attached to the bottom of the Hong vessel." The captain put the headset to his ear and finally spoke. "Admiral Durke, please. This is Commander Sentori, Fifth District. Have a possible urgent matter here. I'll hold, thank you."

The commander placed his hand over the mouthpiece. "The Hong Line captain and crew denied knowing anything about the sub," he said to Christine. "Not clear if everyone believed them. FBI and our Navy, together with the Brits, have been investigating this incident. Question, as I recall, was about what the small sub was designed to do. No one is sure." He then paused.

"Admiral, this is Greg Sentori, nice to speak with you, sir. Look, I'll be short as I don't want to waste your time. My op specialist just came into my office. A clever woman. She caught a fax from Panama advising us that they spotted a Hong Line ship coming out of the Panama Canal. Ship has a small list, but perhaps more importantly, she is riding high, with only half a cargo-load aboard. They thought that unusual given the season. Question is, what do we do with this information? Could be something, could be nothing."

Christine watched for the next five minutes as the commander nodded his head up and down, confirming approval of whatever was being said. Sentori was also taking detailed notes in his cramped small writing.

"Yes, thank you, Admiral. I'll have my ops specialist send that along to your office immediately. And by the way, thank you for the Thanksgiving invitation. I have a feeling our wives will be cooking up a storm." There was a pause, and then he said, "Goodbye."

Her boss seemed a bit lost in thought, and then turned to Christine. "Good job. Not sure if the information is important or not, but there has been activity regarding Hong Lines. The admiral is going to personally look into it. Get a copy of that communication to the admiral's office and mark it urgent for his attention."

"Yes, sir. I'll get it done immediately."

As she headed for the door, the captain cleared his throat and added in his deep voice, "Christine, we don't have any further specific orders at the moment. But I think you should keep a close track of the ship, what was her name… *Wild Pony*. See if you can get a couple of satellite photos of her. I want to know where she is going. Find out which terminals that will be handling her cargo operations at each port and the name of the ship's agents. Make sure we have the necessary people on watch. With Thanksgiving only five days away, I don't want to be shorthanded."

Christine said "Aye, sir," and headed back to her desk. Once again, a good hunch had come to her aide. As she got to the desk, her assistant was already waiting with a handful of papers.

"Ma'am, you're not going to believe this. The FBI, the British Navy, MI5, and probably the CIA, are all involved in this as well. This is major James Bond stuff."

Christine sat at her desk, still reveling in her catch. The master petty officer said, "So I have been told. Now, we need some satellite photos of that ship while she is steaming at sea, and I also need her schedule for the next month. When does she arrive in Savannah, and what other ports in the U.S. is she headed for? We may have to give her a royal welcome when she arrives in U.S. waters." The master chief petty officer started to make some notes in her computer, but stopped and called out to her assistant, "Oh, and before I forget, find out what her draft in the water was while going through the Panama Canal. Check the numbers at both ends of the canal. Something smells."

Chapter 27
New York

Getting information out of the Chinese sources had proved a lot slower than Dalia expected. Either the bureaucracy was just miserably slow or someone was intentionally making sure the requests she was making for trade data between China and North Korea involving coal were moving slower than a snail. The only information that was proving helpful were reports from the Baltic and the Singapore Exchanges that contracts for hiring Hong Line vessels for voyages between North Korea and China were still taking place, and that the freight rate for those voyages was substantially higher than other coal movements in the region. The Chinese subsidiary of Hong Lines, Bei Mei, appeared to have a monopoly on the shipments. The exchanges were between organizations in the maritime industry that maintained freight market information and followed the chartering of commercial vessels. Nothing could be found directly about Bei Mei.

Dalia could feel Tim, the team's associate, leaning over her desk trying to peek at the computer screen. Tim was only a few years out of law school and looked to Joe Barrett as his mentor and guide in the field of maritime law. In spite of his youth, which included a fresh and unshaven face, Tim was well known for his dogged persistence on any task assigned to him, a quality which had earned him a position as a law clerk for a year with a well-known federal judge in Brooklyn.

"Tim," said Dalia with a hint of mystery, "why do you think the Chinese government would pay nearly fifty percent more to have Hong Lines carry their coal? There are so many bulk carriers out there that are hurting in this economy; they would do the job for cost."

"Well, first of all, most of those shipowners would run into U.S. and U.N. sanctions regarding trading with North Korea. The world is definitely stepping up those sanctions, and most shipowners don't want to have their vessels caught anywhere near North Korea. And secondly, China doesn't want to use its own ships for fear of criticism from the U.S. or the U.N. So, I suppose China has to pay Hong Lines more to take the risk. But I still agree with you that a fifty percent margin is a high price for China to pay, and it means that coal from other sources further away, like Australia, is probably still cheaper."

"I don't know," replied Dalia. "Maybe this is a way for North Korea to loan money to Hong Lines. They have China pay Hong Lines an agreed amount more than the charter contract, which comes out of the sale of the coal. The result is that Hong Lines has no recorded bank transactions with North Korea, yet it effectively is getting money that would have gone to North Korea."

"In short, money laundering," said Tim. "Could be. Best explanation I have heard yet."

"Well, I think Joe and Captain Ken have to bring this up with Mr. Hong when they see him tomorrow in Seoul. At the very least, it ought to make him squirm," she explained with some glee.

"Dalia, if you're going to speak to Joe, let him know that I checked the port records. There are two Hong Lines ships now in the U.S., but both are due to leave tomorrow. One heads on to Europe and the other sails back to Korea. However, Hong Lines does have a new ship that will be arriving in Savannah tomorrow. It is expected to go up the East Coast to Norfolk,

Baltimore, and then New York. It will be in US waters for about a week. All three ships appear to be on schedule and nothing unusual that I can see."

Dalia looked up at Tim from her computer with a furrow in her forehead. "If Savannah is the first Port of Call, doesn't the Coast Guard do a major inspection of the cargo ship?"

"Yup. Safety inspection, drugs, stowaways, that sort of thing.

Takes over an hour."

Dalia suddenly had that look of inspiration on her face, the one that Joe always feared. "I think we ought to get one of the investigators in Savannah to go down to the dock and check it out. I mean, you never know."

Tim quickly responded, "Dalia, if Joe says that's a good idea, I'll get someone down there in minutes. But not without Joe's OK. Otherwise, the client could kill me, and there goes my Christmas bonus."

She laughed, and told Tim she would send out an email to Joe for his approval.

Chapter 28
Seoul

The reception area at Hong Lines was designed to look very much like the deck of an old and expensive schooner. The floor was made of mahogany planks, laid at an angle to the wall, and calked between the boards. The walls had the look of painted metal, with the signature garnet-colored stripe of the Hong family. Portholes were installed instead of windows on each of the doors. The ceiling had long strips of wood, painted gleaming white, with brass fixtures hanging on gimbals in case the building should decide to list to one side. In fact, brass fixtures and hardware could be seen everywhere in the room, including a standing binnacle that was once used by a captain to adjust the speed of a vessel. An elderly man in a boiler suit was polishing the brass, which probably provided a full-time job. The reception desk was relatively high, constructed of more mahogany, but highly varnished, with the required brass holding rail running along its entire length. Hong Lines certainly gave the impression of being in tip-top seaworthy shape, which was exactly what it wanted its visitors and customers to believe.

Joe looked at his Oris chronograph watch and realized that Mr. Hong had kept them waiting for more than forty minutes beyond their scheduled appointment. He refused to look upset or show that he was annoyed, as he suspected that Mr. Hong was using the tactic to keep them off-balance, or to just rudely antagonize Joe and Captain Ken. The secretary, a very pretty and tall Korean young lady in a silk cheongsam, a body-hugging tight dress, also colored garnet, did an excellent job of avoiding any eye contact. He saw her pick up her phone and she spoke quietly into the receiver. She put it down, and without looking up, announced that Mr. Hong was ready to meet with the two Americans.

Ken stood, lifting his heavy briefcase, and prepared to walk into Mr. Hong's office. Joe remained seated and nonchalant. He suspected that the entire conference room was being viewed on a monitor somewhere. He refused to entertain the audience. Ken sensed the ruse and sat back down. They both pretended to look at some papers being held by Joe and spoke in whispers.

Another fifteen minutes passed before two young ladies, also dressed in tight, garnet-colored silk dresses, arrived in the reception area and asked the two gentlemen to follow them. Joe took his time putting his papers together, and Ken, playing along, decided to open his briefcase and look for a legal pad. The two ladies were obviously getting impatient, and so was the receptionist who had come out from behind her desk and was urging the men on.

"Mr. Hong is waiting. Please hurry."

Joe responded, without missing a beat, "I am sure he can wait a few more moments. It is important that all of us are equally prepared for this inquisition, I mean interview." He gave his big, white-tooth smile to the receptionist and went back to reading some notes and jotting down some figures. He then whispered something in Ken's ear. Ken whispered back, and they both laughed. At that point, Joe looked the receptionist dead in the eye and said in a slow, ominous tone, "We are now ready for Mr. Hong to meet with us." The receptionist's face flashed an expression of anger for just a brief moment, and then returned to her formula smile. The two men followed the robot dolls down the corridor and into a large conference room.

The room was truly magnificent. The woodwork detail everywhere was first class. Floor to ceiling windows seamlessly lined the length of the room and gave a magnificent view of the Han River. The huge silk Chinese carpet on the marble floor, which contained images of dragons and sea serpents, was probably more than five hundred years old. Other oriental antiques were sunk into cubbyholes in the walls opposite the windows, and the walls themselves were paneled with exotic and matched lacquered woods. Hidden pinpoint lights cast highlights on all the important features in the room. Expensive handmade models of several of the Hong Line vessels were encased in glass and mounted on pedestals. However, the most impressive object in the large room was the massive conference table, which Joe estimated to be at least forty feet long. It was constructed of highly polished black marble, which had small gold flecks seemingly floating on the surface. Inlays of contrasting marble provided an oriental design, which ringed the table near its outer edges. An army of tall, supple black leather chairs surrounded the table.

Papers were already neatly stacked at the near end of the table on the side facing the windows. These were obviously the seats that Mr. Hong and his legal counsel had decided to sit in during the meeting. Indeed, one of the hostesses used her hands to point Joe towards the opposite chair. Joe walked to the chair, paused for a moment as if he was about to sit down, and then silently shook his head. He then looked down to the far end of the table, and with a satisfied expression, slowly walked nearly thirty feet to the opposite end of the table. However, rather than pulling out a chair on the long side of the table, he proceeded to the head chair. Joe assumed the chair was probably the one that Mr. Hong personally sat in during important meetings. Joe wiggled a bit in the leather seat until he felt comfortable. The five men standing at the other end of the room, all apparently lawyers employed by

Mr. Hong, showed signs that ran from surprise to shock as Joe set himself up at the head of the boardroom.

Joe looked up and signaled to his partner to take the seat next to him. "Ken, come on down here. The lighting is better and I don't feel a chill."

After consulting with each other in hushed tones, one of the five lawyers for Mr. Hong walked to the end of the room. "Would you be so kind as to sit where we have designated? Mr. Hong will be arriving momentarily."

Joe slowly looked at his watch and with a sign of disappointment on his face, looked up and simply said, "No."

The middle-aged lawyer was not expecting that answer, nor the resistance to his request, and was obviously taken aback.

"Tell Mr. Hong to either join me at this end of the table, or we can pass notes back and forth on this marble runway. You can also tell Mr. Hong that my courtesies to him ended sixty-five minutes ago when he failed to show the courtesy of being prompt for our meeting. If he does not want to go forward with the meeting, that is fine. We will fly back through London and inform his Insurance Club that he has refused to cooperate with this investigation. As I understand, the insurance company's rules require that the shipowner must fully cooperate with this investigation, and that if the shipowner does not, then the underwriter will cancel his insurance and no other marine insurance company will cover Hong Lines. That means that none of the 227 vessels owned by Mr. Hong will be able to call at most major ports around the world." Joe then paused for a moment before adding, "I guess all he will be left with is carrying coal from North Korea to China. That won't be good for business."

The moment the final words were uttered, the conference room door flew open, and in walked Mr. Hong dressed in a dark, English-tailored business suit with a tie carrying his family colors. His face was flushed and his eyes were opened wide. "You dare come into my home and make threats against me?"

Joe took his time to respond, knowing that the delay, and the mention of North Korea, was now eating at Mr. Hong. "No, Mr. Hong. I didn't come into your home to make threats. I came to your office with the courtesy of being on time, and I have acted cordially towards your staff. But your lack of business courtesy is appalling. If you think ignoring me in the reception area would demonstrate your power and control over our meeting, it has completely failed. Indeed, I have profited from it, as I am paid by the hour – whether you speak to me or not. Ironically, I understand the insurance company will charge your company's account for my services. The longer I must wait, the more you pay me. So, why don't we be civil with one another, sit down, and get this over with?"

Hong's eyes continued to bulge and his chin jutted forward. Surrounded by his garrison of lawyers, he looked at Barrett with simmering anger, and finally muttered, "You are sitting in my chair!"

"Yes, I am," said Joe. "Ask nicely and I will move."

Hong refused to say a word. Finally, one of the senior lawyers looked at Joe and stated, "Mr. Barrett, we would all appreciate it if you would kindly shift your seat so that Mr. Hong can use his traditional chair."

Joe rose, holding his documents, and said, "See, that was not so hard." He then moved from the head of the table around to the right side of the conference table, taking the first seat. Captain Ken immediately sat down next to Joe and began to spread out the files. Mr. Hong walked to the head of the table and stood next to his prized furniture. Seeing that Barrett was not going to stand as a courtesy to him, he slowly lowered himself into the big leather seat. His attorneys waited till he was settled and then took their own positions opposite Barrett.

Chapter 28

Hong stared a cold steel gaze upon Joe Barrett until finally, in a gruff voice, he asked, "Why are you here?

Joe stared back and said, "You know exactly why I am here. I am here to find out about that mystery sub that was attached to your vessel, the *Crazy Horse*, and if there are more subs, and what purpose the subs serve. That is why I am here."

Waving his hand through the air dismissively, Hong replied with contempt, "I know of no submarine. You are wasting your time. Go home."

Ken then handed Joe a half dozen pieces of paper, as he had anticipated the response. "Mr. Hong, if you are going to deny the submarine, then we are going to be here a long time. I can start by demanding the production of all the material on the vessel data recorders, then we will move onto the ship's deck log, the master's personal log, the chief engineers' log, the fuel consumption log, draft and stability calculations, and I have only just begun. Captain Libby here is fully qualified to analyze all those materials." Joe laid the papers in his hand on the table, and then looked around the table. "You know what all that data will tell me? It will show that the *Crazy Horse* was delayed when it left the port of Colon after crossing the Panama Canal and sat for more than an hour at the pilot station after dropping the pilot. Our records show that there was a satellite call from Mr. Hong's personal cell phone to the master on the ship during that interim." Joe lay the first sheet down in front of Mr. Hong, which was a phone record from the SatNav communication service. One of the lawyers picked it up, scanned it with another lawyer, and then handed it to Mr. Hong. He refused to touch it and simply sat with his hands folded together watching Barrett carefully.

"Then, we get to the voyage to Europe," Barrett continued. The ship was making two knots less in speed than its service speed, and less than the speed recommended by the routing service your company uses." Again, Joe handed over another sheet, which the routing company had used to calculate the fuel consumption. "Indeed, it is less than the fuel consumption during the initial part of the voyage from Seoul to Panama." Joe then laid down a third sheet. "Why? Because the *Crazy Horse* picked up the weight of the submarine in Colon, Panama, out at that pilot station. The sub acted as a drag during the cross-Atlantic voyage. Not quite as much as we would have expected, but still enough to be statistically significant, and not due to other factors." Joe handed the lawyer on the other side of the table a fourth sheet of paper with calculations by a naval engineer. "I can only guess, Mr. Hong, that your sub tried to use some propulsion during the voyage to make up for the drag, but they haven't got it fine-tuned yet. Indeed, your office in Long Beach, California, is being served with a subpoena as we sit here demanding to look at the course recorder for the *Crazy Horse* during its last ten voyages." A younger lawyer on the other side of the table suddenly got up and left the room, no doubt to check with the agent.

Joe continued. "I am very certain that the course recorders will show that the ship was steering an erratic path once the sub was attached to the bottom of the Crazy Horse in an effort to compensate for the drag that was only on one side of the ship."

Mr. Hong pushed all the papers back to Joe without looking at any of them. "These papers are of no consequence, Mr. Barrett. They prove nothing about what I know. Even if this mystery sub of your does exist, it does not belong to me."

Joe smiled for the first time and confidently said, "On that, Mr. Hong, we are finally in agreement. The submarine obviously belongs to North Korea." Joe paused long enough for the comment to sink in. Hong's expression remained frozen, but his left hand twitched. Joe continued, "The vessel is used for transporting drugs and laundering money. We know that because cocaine and traces of $100 bills have been found in the sub that was attached to your ship. Hong Lines is nothing more than a mother vessel that transports the subs, unseen and undetectable, from one port to another."

Hong's attorneys leaned over to counsel Mr. Hong. The old man raised his left hand to stop them, and then leaned forward to gaze directly at Barrett. "That is a very serious allegation, Mr. Barrett. One that could get you put in jail here in Korea because you have no evidence to back it up, or perhaps even worse. Unless you have something in your briefcase that shows that my company is connected to this underwater ship, I suggest you leave now before I ask my legal staff to take action."

"Mr. Hong, I have already been threatened many times in my investigation of this matter, of which I am sure you are aware, so I take my statements very seriously. So does your insurance company, and so does the U.S. government, the British government, Interpol, and others. I hear that even the Korean government is beginning to take an interest in your activities."

Hong stood, indicating that he had heard enough. The lawyers next to him helped pull out the chair.

Then, Joe off-handedly commented, "I guess you don't want to discuss Bei Mei? Or perhaps Geulimja – did I pronounce that correctly? The shadow? By the way, how is he doing?"

The Chairman looked like he had a stroke. He pushed the hands of his lawyers away from him and brusquely sat. He asked for a glass of water and then looked at Joe. "What do those words mean?"

"Actually, I was hoping that you could tell me. Best as I can tell, Bei Mei is your shell company in China, which arranges for the carriage of coal from North Korea to northern Chinese ports using Hong Lines ships that are supposedly laid up. I understand that Bei Mei is paid handsomely by Korea for the use of your ships, or, at least, that is what BIMCO reports. I don't need to give you that sheet."

"What proof do you have my ships are transporting cargo to North Korea?"

Joe quickly responded, "Not to North Korea; rather *from* North Korea. China gets the coal it needs for its factories in the north, North Korea gets the money it needs to develop its weapons. But that's not quite enough for North Korea's chairman. By selling drugs from China, North Korea has gained a lot more cash flow. And, as for Hong Lines, it gets a lot of unseen cash from carrying the coal and protecting the subs, which, as far as our forensic accountant can determine, you desperately need to keep the company running. Without that cash, your empire would be bust."

Everyone stared at Mr. Hong, whose face had turned stone cold. He stood up again, without the assistance of his lawyers, and with his hands on the edge of the table, he announced, "Goodbye, Mr. Barrett. Our time is over. I wish you a pleasant stay in Seoul. But be careful, Korea can be a dangerous place. I will advise the London insurance company that I have completed my cooperation. Good day." The portly old man walked at a deliberately slow pace out of the conference room followed by all his lawyers, except one – the young lawyer who had run out of the conference room after Joe had mentioned the subpoena. Joe closed his bag and looked up at the youthful lawyer who was obviously there to make sure they left. He turned to Ken and whispered, "I guess they don't trust us with their pretty women or their antiques." Captain Ken laughed and headed towards the conference room door. The lawyer pointed the way to the elevator lobby. As they got in the elevator, the lawyer joined them. Joe looked over and said, "Did you check on that subpoena? Federal rules give you ten days to respond. My office will be waiting. Here's my card if you want to call me about the other subpoenas that will be coming in the next few days. Should make you busy and give you a lot of billable hours. Maybe you will even get a bonus at the end of the year."

The young lawyer did not smile or comment. As Joe and Ken exited the elevator on the ground floor, the lawyer held the door open and simply stated, "Mr. Hong has offered you his limousine to get back to your hotel. I think this driver won't get lost like the last one." His lips parted just enough to hint at a smile.

"Don't like the tone of that," Ken said to Joe, watching the attorney get back into the elevator.

"Nor I. Would almost suggest we head straight to the airport, except for my clothing and files at the hotel. I am getting tired of having to arrange for hotels to ship my luggage back to New York."

As they left security and headed through the huge revolving doors of the skyscraper, Joe noticed that two very large men approached him in a pincer move. They grabbed Joe by his elbows and pushed him forward. Joe attempted to protest but felt something poking him hard in the ribs. He looked down and could just see the glint of what was definitely the barrel of a pistol aimed towards his kidney. Joe looked over his shoulder and realized that Captain Ken was in the same predicament and was being escorted by another set of goons. They steered both men towards a black Mercedes van waiting at the curb. The rear door slid open and Joe and Ken were both hurled into the truck. Joe landed on his shoulder and immediately felt a stabbing pain. Ken landed against the far wall of the van and bounced off the steel panel. Heavy bags were pulled over their heads. Both Joe and Ken had their arms twisted behind their backs and their hands secured with plastic ties. They were then thoroughly searched. Their phones were taken out of their pockets. Joe yelled out, "Hey, what the hell do you think you are doing?" There was no response. Joe again remarked, "Mr. Hong is going to get you into major problems with the police. You are not going to get away with this." The only response was a hushed snicker that was cut short by a hard slap to the back of Joe's head.

The slap was totally unexpected, and under the hood, Joe was beginning to feel disoriented and alone. He called out to Ken, "You alright Ken?" A fist immediately smashed into the side of Joe's jaw. Blood began to trickle down Joe's split lip.

Captain Ken responded, "Yeah, I'm good." A heavy boot caught Ken in the stomach, and he bent over in pain and groaned. The message was clear. No talking.

The van moved fast, swaying around corners and accelerating down long stretches. Both Joe and Ken tried to concentrate on the turns and the background sounds to get an idea of where they were being taken. After what seemed like more than an hour of driving, the van turned hard and uphill onto an unpaved road. The vehicle began thumping and slewing over what must have been a dirt surface. The van then slowed to a crawl, but still the ride was filled with potholes and mounds. After a sharp turn to the left, they came to a stop. The van door could be heard sliding back, and enough light now filtered through the fabric hood that Joe could tell there was still daylight. No words were used as the two Americans were pushed out of the vehicle without warning, falling prone onto a gravel surface.

Ken called out, "Hey, Joe! You still there?" A second later, he was again kicked in the back with enough force that even Joe could hear the impact. Ken grunted but did not cry out in pain.

Both men were then picked up off the ground and forced to walk forward. Joe felt the gun pressed into his ribcage once more. A huge hand on his shoulder navigated his direction. After thirty or forty steps, they came to a stop. The sound of a large garage door opener could be heard and a metal door somewhere in front of them was mechanically being lifted up. When the noise stopped, Joe and Ken were again pushed forward. They walked into what Joe suspected was a huge warehouse, as the sound pattern changed, and even their footsteps seemed to be followed by echoes. The temperature also got colder.

Both Americans were forced to sit on the floor. Their hoods were removed, but not their cuffs. Joe could immediately see they were indeed in a warehouse that was filled with tens of thousands of crates of what appeared to be fruits and vegetables. The crates were still stacked on pallets, and the stencils on some of the crates showed they had come from South America, the U.S., and Indonesia. Joe concluded that they must have been in a distribution center located near a pier that handles vessels carrying cargo from overseas. But he still had no idea where in Korea they were located. Two men in dark suits with dark glasses stood very still in front of them holding pistols. Then, a third man walked into the warehouse, dressed in an expensive dark-blue suit. He was one of the senior lawyers that Hong had sitting next to him in the conference room. He stood directly in front of them.

"Now I ask the questions," he said with a hiss. "Who sent you here?"

Joe responded with as level a voice as he could maintain, "You know who sent us here. East of England, the marine insurance company. Mr. Hong received a letter from them over a week ago requesting this meeting, and he agreed to it."

Without warning, Captain Ken was again kicked in the ribs by the guard in front of him. A 'pop' sound suggested at least one rib was broken. He bent over and threw up.

"Why the hell did you kick him if I am answering the questions?" screamed Joe.

"Because you have the answers. We need to keep you alive for those answers. Now, once again, who sent you here? Don't give me the same answer or your friend will have another rib broken. Which government sent you?"

Joe looked around the room, the glass windows blinding him with the sunlight from the setting sun. He could hear Ken moan from the pain.

"We came here at the instructions of the insurance company, but before you kick my friend again, the FBI came to our office early this week and met with us about Hong Shipping. They know we are here to see Mr. Hong."

"Now that wasn't so hard, was it?" the Korean lawyer sneered, copying the phrase that Joe had used on Mr. Hong in the conference room. "Which Hong Lines vessels are they tracking now?"

Joe looked up, not expecting the question. "Huh?" he responded. "How would I know which ships the U.S. government is tracking?"

This time, the kick was to Joe's back, near the kidney. Joe rolled up like a ball in pain and collapsed flat on the floor, blood seeping out of his mouth. He looked over at Ken, who was also lying flat on the concrete, apparently nearly passed out from the pain. Joe squinted one eye to look up at the lawyer, who appeared to be finally amused. Suddenly, the attorney's head froze in mid-laugh and bent slightly backward. A red dot on his forehead expanded and began to ooze blood down over his eyebrows. His eyes were frozen. The lawyer's knees buckled and he fell onto his bloodied face. Joe looked over at the two guards, who were obviously caught by surprise. Suddenly, a portion of the back of the head of the man standing over Ken flew off, and what was left of him was thrown backward. Ken twisted to see the watchman who was guarding him, and turned just in time to see his face explode into bits and pieces, with blood spraying out everywhere. He slumped to the ground, falling on what was left of his head.

"Shit," was all that Joe could think to say as he saw the stream of blood from the two bodies eddy its way towards him.

Chapter 28

"What happened?" said Captain Ken with a horse and shallow voice.

"Bad guys – all dead. Not sure what happens to us. Maybe someone thinks we are already dead because we are on the floor."

"No need to worry, I won't be getting up soon," he tried to joke, but with a stab of pain from his broken rib causing him to cough.

The pounding of boots on the cement floor caught their ears as a group of people ran toward them. Joe closed his eyes, deciding to pretend he was dead. At this point, there was enough blood on him and under him to make it convincing.

"Ken, are you hurt?" whispered someone with a British accent.

Joe immediately recognized the sweet voice of Yeoman Fox.

"I'm fine, thanks for asking," said Joe as he rolled over. He smiled up at Fox, although the image was ghastly as he was smeared in dark red blood, and even his white teeth had streaks of blood from the broken lip. He nodded his head towards Ken. "Seriously, Ken is hurt; at least one broken rib. What the hell took you guys so long? I thought you were listening to us all the time on that chip?"

"They took your phones and put them in a taxi," she said. "We followed the phones for nearly a half hour until we realized it was a goose chase. Then, we had to triangulate the chip, which was just at the edge of its reception. We got lucky and managed to find your transmission from one of our patrol boats in the river."

For the first time, she was not in a skirt or dress but instead wearing military combat fatigues. "You are in Inchon," she said, "a commercial port just west of Seoul on the Han. There are a lot of warehouses in this section. We figured out which warehouse when we saw Mr. Hong's car parked in front of this one. Luckily, it had windows that our snipers could see through, although, with the setting sun I doubt you could see us. When we saw that you were both down on the ground, I gave the order to shoot."

She then directed the small force of military men to help Joe and Ken to their feet and carry them out to the waiting truck. A medic gave Ken an injection to relieve the pain. Joe stumbled on his first two steps but was able to get his balance back. He could hear Fox giving orders to dispose of the bodies, clean up the floor, and dump the van and car. There had to be no sign that anyone ever came into the warehouse that day.

By the time they drove off the terminal, Joe's face had been cleaned up enough that he looked alive and human. Captain Ken was coming around, and the medic had placed bandages around his waist to hold his rib cage together. Large dark blue bruises could be seen on his back and stomach.

Fox came over and sat on the bench next to Joe. "Really sorry about that, Mr. Barrett. We didn't intend for you fellows to get hurt. But Mr. Hong is obviously panicking and showing his nasty side."

"His lawyer, the guy you shot, was asking me if you were tracking any of Hong's vessels? Why? The only thing I can think of is that he must be concerned that one of his ships has a Pilot Fish attached and is being tracked."

"Exactly our reaction." I have already passed that along to the FBI and Interpol. We have our people working on it now. As for you and Captain Ken, the plan is to get you out of Korea and back home safely. You understand I can't take you back to the hotel. We are taking you to a U.S. military base where you will be flown back to New York."

"I don't know why I bother bringing luggage on these trips," quipped Joe. "It always ends up being shipped home without me." He smiled. "Can I borrow your phone. I suspect there is a lady back in New York who is going to be very upset with me."

As Fox handed him her phone she looked at him with compassion. "She already knows, Joe. We have been keeping her informed. I think she understands."

Chapter 29
Savannah

The Korean captain of the *Wild Pony* had more than twenty years' experience, but every time he entered U.S. waters, it caused him a pang of fear. He knew the U.S. Coast Guard was always watching his ships with high-powered optics on their satellites; through the video lenses of drones that continuously circled far overhead, and through the binoculars of sailors on the vessels stationed outside of the entrance to the Savannah River, a tributary that ran 301 miles into the Appalachian Mountains. While many other nations had Coast Guard services, the United States Coast Guard had far more advanced technology, equipment, experienced men, and gun power than any other country he had visited. While he understood that the Coast Guard served a good and humane purpose by rescuing people at sea and assisting when there were marine catastrophes and emergencies in any ocean, the fact of the matter was that the "coasties" were treating every foreign vessel that came into U.S. waters as carrying possible terrorists or weapons. The Coast Guard was now part of Homeland Security and they took their job seriously. While the captain did not believe that there was any reason to single out his vessel, there was something odd about this voyage from the start. His vessel had been traveling with an uncorrectable list and unexplained fuel consumption. He heard that those conditions were rumored to have existed on the *Crazy Horse* before the incident in the English Channel. Now, everyone was keeping their eye on

Hong Lines' ships. He even heard that Captain Park had died in his sleep shortly after the incident. Very strange things were happening, indeed.

The first port of call in the United States for a foreign vessel always involved a fairly thorough inspection of the entire ship by the Coast Guard. A team of inspectors combed the ship, checking everything from safety equipment, to stowaways, drugs, oil spills, and proper record keeping. Captain Ree didn't want any troubles, and had pushed his crew for two days after leaving the Panama Canal to make sure that every inch of the ship passed inspection. As the container ship tied up at her berth in Savannah, the captain gave the signal to lower the gangway. There were three Coast Guard men in their blazing international orange work suits already standing by the string piece. However, to his surprise, there was also a Coast Guard officer, a woman of medium height with dark black hair, wearing a dark blue uniform with stripes on the sleeve. She carried a briefcase, which was most unusual. His heart raced a bit.

The moment the gangway hit the tarmac on the pier, the three men, clad in orange, were up the swaying ladder in seconds. A crewman had already been posted as a guard at the ship's rail, as required, to ensure that no one came on board until the Coast Guard had finished their inspection. The three inspectors forked off in different directions, heading to the bridge, the engine room, and the cargo decks to do their respective jobs. The senior officer took her time walking up the ladder, not because of the angle of the climb but rather because she continually stopped to stare down at the waterline and then up towards the bridge. Captain Ree walked aft from the midship house and met the officer as she neatly came over the rail onto the main deck. The captain held out his hand to greet the woman.

"Master Chief Petty Officer Milagros," Christine introduced herself. "I am the Operations Specialist with the Fifth District."

The captain slightly bowed, and then said, "I am Captain Ree, Master of this vessel. How may I help you?"

"We received a rather strange report that your vessel left Colon with a list to port, by about five degrees. I understand you spoke with the Captain of the Port, Garcia, concerning the situation."

"Yes, ma'am. I spoke with him directly by ship radio. We told him we would try to correct the problem once at sea. As you can see the vessel has no list at this point."

"Well, that's good to hear. When did you correct the problem?"

The captain was silent for a moment as he thought. The fact of the matter was that her list only corrected itself mysteriously this morning as they entered the channel to come into the Savannah River. But if he said that, it meant he crossed the Gulf of Mexico with an improper ballast. "I think we corrected it a few hours after we dropped the pilot in Colon. All is good now."

"The problem with that, Captain Ree, is that our patrol boat observed you fifty miles off the coast of Georgia this morning and it still seemed you had a list. Can we go take a look at your VDR recordings up on the bridge and see what the problem is? You are aware that these lists can prove to be very dangerous in storms, resulting in cargo falling off the ship, crew getting injured, and even vessels capsizing." The last part was not a question but a direct statement from the Coast Guard Officer.

As they headed towards the bridge, the captain was obviously getting nervous. The VDR recording would prove he had lied. He turned to the Master Petty Officer and said, "I may have been mistaken. We have been adjusting our ballast at several points to correct the problem. I and the chief engineer are uncertain why the ship would not properly respond to the extra seawater pumped into the bilge to correct the list. However, I am certain that the list is now corrected and the ship is at the correct sailing angle."

"Captain, I am pleased that you are being honest with me. But it still does not answer the questions of why you had a list, and as you just indicated, neither you or your engineer could solve the problem. My job is to make sure that this vessel goes to sea safe and sound, and that we avoid any risk of life to the sailors or damage to the cargo. So, let me take a look at the recordings and see if we can figure this out together."

When they reached the bridge, the chief mate was filling in logbooks and checking stow plans against the cargoes being discharged. He was surprised to see the female Coast Guard Officer enter the bridge area; that could only mean one thing—trouble.

"Officer Milagros, this is my chief officer, Lee. Mr. Lee, the Coast Guard is investigating why our ship had a list of five degrees during the voyage to Savannah."

"Actually, Captain, our reports are that the *Wild Pony* was at a list when she went into the Panama Canal as well."

Lee looked up and smiled, "But the problem is fixed. No more list now."

Christine studied the chief officer's face. "So, how did you correct the problem, and why couldn't it be fixed earlier?"

The chief mate and the captain looked at each other, obviously without an explanation.

"Let me guess," said Milagros, "the problem fixed itself?"

Captain Ree, realizing they were in dangerous territory with the Coast Guard, decided to respond truthfully. The ship's records would prevent them from lying and only get them fined by the Coast Guard for being untruthful.

"The chief mate is correct. As we took on the pilot to come into Savannah, the ship corrected its list, and the problem has not returned. We did not make any adjustments."

"Chief," said the master petty officer, "you are in charge of cargo operations, am I correct?"

"Yes, ma'am. I am the cargo officer."

"I noticed from the manifest that your ship is only carrying about 62 percent of the maximum cargo, whereas every other container ship coming in from the Far East is nearly 100 percent filled. Why is your ship so light on cargo?"

"I cannot answer that question. I do not get involved in deciding which cargoes this ship carries. That decision is made directly by the company office in Seoul."

"But you agree with me that, at this time of year, the vessels you have sailed on in the past are generally full?"

"Yes, that is true. But no one tells me why we have fewer containers on this voyage."

"Captain, when was the last time a diver checked the bottom of your ship?"

Captain Ree was caught in utter surprise by this question and his face showed the shock. The chief mate was equally perplexed. "I don't think there is anything wrong with the ship bottom. The vessel was in dry dock about sixteen months ago."

The chief petty officer pulled out her cell phone and dialed in some numbers. "Even so, we need to check it since there is no explanation for list or the cure of the list problem. We will use our divers. Please make sure you give them full cooperation. The ship must remain at her berth until the operation is completed. I don't think it will take more than a couple of hours. Meanwhile, Chief, I would like you to download your loading and stability calculations to my office this morning. Here is my card. Hopefully, this all proves to be nothing, but my job is to make sure it is nothing." As she left the bridge, she could be heard giving orders to have the Coast Guard send divers to check and photograph the bottom.

Captain Ree quickly ran into the radio room and arranged for an email to be sent to the head office, attention Mr. Hong, about what had just happened.

Chapter 30
Atlantic Ocean

Jian was not happy with the idea of going up the Savannah River. He had a bad premonition. While the presence of the Savannah Nuclear Reactor plant was only a few hundred meters from the river's edge, and about halfway to the city center, making it a perfect place to drop one of the bombs, the Savannah port pilot was insisting that the *Wild Pony* go up river to the port of Savannah at low tide because of the ship's low draft. The lack of cargo was now creating a problem for Jian because, at low tide, the river would only provide about four-foot clearance below the keel of the sub. That was too little margin for comfort. If the submarine hit a rock or object on the bottom of the river while attached to the underside of the container ship, it would be torn to shreds. He had heard stories of how an abandoned anchor on the bottom of the Delaware River had split open the hull of an oil tanker many years ago, leaving the ship to sink on the spot. The captain, in that case, thought he had three feet of clearance from the bottom of the river.

Jian finally ordered Bae to unlatch the sub from the *Wild Pony* just as the pilot came on board off the mouth of the Savannah River. They still had the ports of Norfolk and New York to drop the two bombs. The Chairman insisted that at least one bomb was planted near Washington, D.C. – that meant Norfolk. Norfolk was a deep port and would not present any problems. The U.S. Navy had its largest concentration of military vessels there.

Even if it was nearly two hundred miles from the Capitol, the fallout would also have its toll in Washington.

The key target, thought Jian, was the port of New York. The center of America's corrupt financial wealth and economic control over the world would be crushed. This time, it would be much more effective than just toppling the World Trade Center. He said nothing to Bae. His partner was becoming more and more sullen and quiet. When the time actually came, there might be a problem following orders. He would have to be prepared for that unfortunate circumstance.

All they had to do was sit quietly and wait for the *Wild Pony* to drop her pilot after exiting the Savannah River. They would then catch a ride to Norfolk.

Chapter 31
Pyongyang

The Chairman smiled as he looked in the mirror at his new suit. Custom made in Hong Kong, it had cost over three thousand dollars – enough to feed a small village for over a year – but that was of no consequence. What was important is that his people believed their Chairman looked prosperous; that way, they would believe that they, too, must be prospering. What else did they have to believe in? The tailor pulled on the waist of the jacket, which irritated the Chairman as it reminded him that he was somewhat portly, and not like the tall, trim, athletic men that graced the covers of all the movie magazines. When the tailor tried to pull down the left trouser leg to have it crease just right on the surface of the rich Italian shoe, the head of state of North Korea kicked the tailor, sending him sprawling over the gleaming wood floor. The frightened tailor hid his eyes from the leader, picked up his tools, and ran out of the office. The Chairman only grinned before picking an apple out of a large fruit bowl and polishing it on the sleeve of his new, grey, mohair suit jacket.

On his desk was a message from Bei Mei. It revealed that Mr. Hong had received an email from the captain of the *Wild Pony.* Apparently, a female officer from the US Coast Guard had boarded the ship in Savannah and warned the captain that they were going to do an underwater inspection of the vessel. "Huh," he thought. *A female officer in the Coast Guard giving an order to a ship captain.* "Ridiculous." Well, they would not find anything. The pilot of his sub had sent an encrypted message by satellite that he had decided not to go up the Savannah River for fear of grounding in the low tide. He was waiting in the Atlantic. The Chairman chuckled. He was so much brighter than the stupid Americans. Soon, there would be "fire and fury" like their president predicted, albeit in their own backyard. And they wouldn't know who to blame for the nuclear blasts.

The young Chairman sat at his desk and took out a pen and a sheet of paper. Mr. Hong was getting to be a problem. He knew too much, and the latest report from his spies confirmed that he had once again failed to kill the American lawyers. There was really no more need for Mr. Hong.

Chapter 32
New York

Dalia laid quietly in bed, the moonlight peeking through the blinds providing just enough illumination to see the ugly dark-blue bruise, in the shape of a boot's toe, above the waist on Joe's bare back. As he turned in his restless sleep, she could see other whelps on his arm and torso. At least he did not have any broken bones, like poor Ken. She gently placed her hand on Joe's shoulder and ran it down to his chest. Hopefully, he would sleep the entire night. As she stroked the hair over his ear, Dalia suddenly realized that she was looking into one of Joe's blue eyes. He was now awake and watching her. He allowed a slow grin to part his lips.

"Can't sleep? Tried counting sheep?" said Joe in a husky whisper.

"Actually, I thought I would count the bruises on your back. I am pretty sure there are more there than sheep on a farm." Her answer maintained a serious tone.

"They'll heal." Joe saw the glint in Dalia's eye and quickly realized that was not the right response. "And I promise never to go back to Korea. In fact, have I told you how much more comfortable this bed is than a metal bench seat on a C-5 transport? The Air Force has no stewardesses, movies, or even pillows, and the drinks are all non-alcoholic. I refuse to fly with them again." Joe rolled on his side so that he could watch her with both eyes. Dalia's hair was short. It crept over her forehead and left her pixie ears showing. He could see that she wanted to be serious, but he wasn't going to start that conversation at three in the morning. He used his fingers to brush her hair to the side, kissed her on the cheek, and said in his most serious voice, "Let's talk tomorrow. Tonight, let's be glad we have one another." As he started to close his eyes and drift off, he could feel Dalia pulling him towards her and pressing her body into his.

* * *

Joe entered the reception room of Hooper & Kingsley looking much more refreshed and feeling a lot fewer aches. However, no sooner had he came out of the elevator doors than the young receptionist pointed towards the managing partner's office. She shook her head, indicating that Mr. Allister J. McDonald was waiting to see him. Joe could only imagine the lecture he was about to receive from the old and crusty senior partner of the firm. Joe knocked twice on the door after getting the signal from McDonald's secretary to go on in.

"Joe, come on in. Take a seat." McDonald pushed away the papers on his desk and rose to his feet to greet Barrett. "How are you feeling? Heard you took quite a beating overseas, and I understand that literally?"

"Doing fine, sir. Couple of more days and I should be able to run a marathon."

"Joe, you didn't run the marathon before you went to Korea. I don't expect this recent trip will now have you running it." McDonald sat back in his chair. "Joe, this is serious stuff you and Mr. Libby have gotten into. I received a call from the FBI and a, what was her name, a Ms. Fox from the British embassy, both thanking you for your efforts overseas. They seem to think some good results will come from… whatever you two did over there."

"Well, that was very kind of them, sir. But the fact is that they did more for us than we did for them."

"Not sure what that means, Joe, and I am not certain I want to know. The reason I called you in is to tell you to take a little more time off to recuperate. Same for Mr. Libby. I don't want you fellows pushing yourselves."

"Thank you, Mr. McDonald. But the fact is that we both want to get back to work and focus on the future."

"Very glad to hear that, Joe. It will be good to get things back on an even keel – isn't that what you maritime lawyers call it?" He chuckled wittingly. "And maybe you can focus a little more on your intentions with Dalia. I've received some very impressive evaluations on her work."

"Thank you, sir. In fact, I think you should be one of the first to know that I will be proposing to her. Your blessing is important to us."

"You've got it, son. Now, back to work, if that's what you want. Good to see you have returned." McDonald went back to the stack of papers on his desk, signaling that the meeting was over.

Joe walked slowly back to his office. The invitation to take some time off actually sounded good; his back was still very sore. However, the vision of Hong's lawyer pressing him as to whether the government was following any of Hong's ships kept playing over and over in his head. The lawyer was not interested in whether Joe was following the ships, only what the government was doing. That had to mean something serious was being planned, and something current. Hong wouldn't take the risk of killing him and Captain Ken unless something was already in progress. And if his guess was right, there was a bomb on its way to somewhere in the United States. The only way to find it was to locate the Pilot Fish. And the only way to find the Pilot Fish was to track the mother ship. *So, which of Hong's ships is the mother ship?*

Chapter 32

By the time Joe reached his office door, he had a hundred thoughts swirling in his head. Dalia was already there with a cup of coffee in her hand. So were Captain Ken and his associate Tim.

"Is anyone tracking Hong Line vessels coming to the U.S.?" Joe asked.

Ken, still bandaged around the chest, looked up with wide eyes. "Joe, you're kidding aren't you? We're out of the Hong case. We should be preparing for the trial in the new fire case."

Dalia also spoke up. "Come on, Joe. You guys were nearly killed. This is way over your head. Let the Army or Navy, whatever, take care of it."

"Look," said Joe sharply, "I'm not stopping the military or anyone else from going after Hong Line or the Pilot Fish. My fear is that there is not much time left before some part of the U.S. gets blown off the map. And I would bet my bottom dollar that New York is going to be ground zero." He stared at each of them. "I'm not talking about us running in with guns blazing. I'm just talking about finding the Pilot Fish. That's the key. Find the sub and let the Navy, Coast Guard, or whatever, do their job. So far, we have been way out in front of everyone else in putting the big picture together. I wouldn't want to think that, if a bomb went off in my home town, that I might have been able to prevent it." He looked around the room once more, his eyes hard and dark. "Are we in this together?"

"OK, Joe, all we are doing is trying to locate where the Pilot Fish is. But I'm getting a bit old to use karate on thugs," smiled Capt. Ken.

Dalia was quiet and so was Tim. They knew they had no choice but to support Joe.

"Tim, you have that software that tracks cargo ships on your computer, right? Can you program it to track all of the Hong Line ships that are coming to America?"

"Already did, boss. Somehow I had a feeling this was going to come up. There are three of Hong's vessels headed to the U.S. One is the *Happy Horse*. She is in Long Beach and heading next to Vancouver and then back to Korea. But it's a relatively small vessel, carrying only twenty-five hundred containers. Not sure they would use something that small to hide the Pilot Fish."

Tim flipped a page in his notebook. "Next one is the *White Mustang* and she is scheduled to enter the Panama Canal in two days before heading onto Port Arthur and Mobile. The last one, here it is, the *Wild Pony*, is berthed in Savannah and headed to Norfolk, Baltimore, and then New York." He looked up at Joe.

"That's the ship. Bet on it. The *Wild Pony*. What do we know about her?"

"One of the newer vessels in Hong's fleet. Fourteen-thousand containers. Pretty big. Service speed twenty-two knots. Crew of eighteen. Captain's name is Ree."

Joe thought for a second. "And when does she get to Norfolk and New York?"

"She'll be in Norfolk in two days and New York in five. How come you didn't ask about Baltimore?"

"The Chesapeake is too shallow. The sub won't risk going into Baltimore, but Norfolk is one of the deepest harbors in the U.S. That's why the Navy is there, and New York has been recently dredged to about fifty feet in depth. The sub wouldn't need to go all the way into Port Newark. Easier to drop the bomb right in New York's harbor."

Joe swiveled in his chair and brought up the contacts list on his computer. "Who were those Coast Guard officers we were dealing with when we had the stowaway case?"

Dalia cleared her throat. "Lt. Commander Brain McLee. There was also the younger fellow, John Oakely, who was a maritime law enforcement specialist."

Chapter 32

"Oakley, that's the guy. I think McLee is too high up the chain for us, but Oakley would probably listen. Dalia, can you find his phone number and let's give him a call?" Five minutes later, Joe was on the speakerphone with John Oakley.

"Mr. Oakley, this is Joe Barrett. Perhaps you remember me from the incident involving the two children who were stowaways on the *m/v Dana* last year?"

"Yes, Joe. I remember you and your team very well. What can I do for you? No more stowaways, I hope."

"Ah, no. No stowaways, more like possible bombs this time." There was silence on the other end, and then Oakley said, "Bombs?

You're kidding, of course."

"Nope. Fact is that I have been helping British MI5 and the FBI on an investigation regarding a highly developed small sub that attaches to the bottom of vessels that can sneak in and out of ports."

"Frankly, I wouldn't normally believe you, Joe. However, I just got a memo yesterday advising Coast Guard districts to be on the lookout for these mini-subs. What do you know about them?"

"You remember my paralegal, Captain Ken? Well, we started off being invited by London marine insurers to view a very advanced, miniature, mystery sub that was attached to the *Crazy Horse* cargo ship that had a collision last month in the English Channel. The sub is now secured at a naval base in Southampton, England. We got up real close to the vessel and even got inside it. Then, I visited the maker of the unique hydro-magnetic engines in Genoa, Italy. A few days ago, both Ken and I were in Korea to discuss the matter with Hong Lines. That didn't go well and we were abducted in Seoul; that is, until the British special services broke us out. We think Hong Lines is providing cover for the submarines in exchange for receiving higher than normal freight rates from China. China, in turn, is being compensated by North Korea, which is providing shipments of coal, probably at no charge. China built the subs for North Korea and is now being paid for their construction by North Korea with the cash that the subs are generating by transporting and selling drugs. Now, our fear is that North Korea will use their advanced mini-sub to sneak a bomb or bombs into U.S. ports."

"Shit, Joe. Why are you telling me this stuff? You should be telling the FBI."

"Already have. And they are working on it with Homeland Security. But my associate discovered that there is a ship owned by Hong Lines called the *Wild Pony,* which is currently berthed in Savannah, and afterward, will head to Norfolk and New York. A matter of days. I have a hunch that a North Korean sub is attached to that container ship."

"Why that ship?"

"Only three days ago, Hong Lines tried to be very persuasive in asking Ken and myself if we know whether our government is now tracking any of their ships. And the only Hong vessel that is large enough to hide a sub, and is coming into major U.S. ports, is the *Wild Pony*. We just want to find out if anyone from your branch has inspected the ship in Savannah. I think someone should send a diver down and inspect her bottom. Couldn't do any harm."

Again, Oakley paused. "That's a pretty tall order, Joe. I can't order divers, but let me call the Coast Guard's Fifth District commander and see what they know about this vessel. Give me your number and I'll get back to you."

A couple of minutes later, Joe hung up the phone, satisfied that they were off to a good start. He then looked over and saw Dalia's face go white. She was staring at her phone. She looked up and softly said, "Just got a news alert. Mr. Hong is dead. They think it's a heart attack. He was slumped over his desk in his office. This doesn't sound good."

"I think someone just moved up the timetable for the Pilot Fish," Joe commented.

Chapter 33
Savannah

The pictures were a bit murky due to the mud and silt in the fast running Savannah River, but there was no doubt that the bottom of the *Wild Pony* did not have a submarine attached to it. Master Chief Petty Officer Milagros kept staring at the monitor in her office, certain that she had missed something while looking at the photos. She had felt so confident that a sub was attached to that container ship. As she continued to bounce the rubber tip of her pencil off of the desktop, Christine saw her assistant, Roseann, walking by her office. She called out and asked her to step in. Roseann had a good eye for detail and seemed to be filled with endless tidbits of knowledge about ships.

"Take a look at these photos taken by the divers," Milagros said. "Definitely no submarine attached. But something strikes me as odd, and I just can't figure out what it is. I have been staring at these photos for over an hour and I'm going cross-eyed."

The assistant looked over her shoulder and peered at the photos, one by one. The monitor provided very good resolution, but the diver's strobe light, particles in the water, and some passing jetsam gave the impression there was a thin gauze over the camera lens.

"Don't see anything, Ma'am. Just a lot of scratches and chips to the bottom paint. Maybe she hit a sand bar? Anyway, she is going to need new bottom paint soon or there will be a lot of barnacles growing on her hull."

Christine looked again at the photos, staring at the scratches on the ship's steel hull. The *Wild Pony* was less than a year old. Why should there be chips in the special formula bottom paint applied by the builder's yard? She executed a couple of steps with her mouse and highlighted an area of the picture, which was then magnified by five times. The missing paint actually had a pie-shaped appearance to it. It was not irregular, nor in a longitudinal stretched shape, which she would expect from a ship which had scraped the river bottom. In fact, as she blew up and focused on each of the scratches, it was clear they were all the same size and all had the same pie-shaped outline. Eight spots, she counted. Christine then rotated the picture to a different angle and pulled a ruler out of her drawer. It wasn't very scientific, but she was pretty certain that the distance between the pie-shaped abrasions in the bottom paint were all the same, running in two rows, with four spots on each side. That was definitely not the pattern of an accidental grounding; this was something man-made. She highlighted each of the marks with a yellow circle that ran outside of the chipped paint, and then forwarded the PDFs to her commander by e-mail. Christine waited two minutes and then picked up the phone to call Captain Greg Santori.

"Captain, this is Christine. I just sent you some underwater photos taken by the diver who went under the hull of the *Wild Pony* in Savannah."

"Yes, I am just opening your email. Did they find a sub attached?" "No, sir, there was no submarine attached to the cargo vessel. But, sir, if you would take a look at the photos, there is something very odd. There are eight pie-shaped, evenly spaced spots or markings on the bottom of the ship. In each instance, the bottom paint has been scraped away. I have circled them. This is a new ship, Captain, and the bottom paint should last for years. That's not the pattern you get from a grounding. They are evenly spaced and almost perfectly triangular in shape. It's something man-made. The

British report that we got on the sub attached to the bottom of the *Crazy Horse* in the English Channel stated that it had some sort of legs that magnetically secured themselves to the bottom of the container ship. Perhaps these are the markings left behind by those legs?"

"Funny you should ask, Christine. I just got off the phone with a John Oakley, who is with maritime law enforcement in our New York office. He says he was just contacted by some lawyers who were hired to investigate the sub, and have been helping the FBI and the Brits. The lawyers say they also think a sub is attached to the *Wild Pony*, and that it is carrying a bomb. I know it sounds crazy, but Oakley says these guys know a lot about the situation, and they even saw one of the subs in England. Why don't you give them a call?"

A few minutes later, Christine Milagros was engaged in a detailed and serious phone conversation with Joe Barrett. She was impressed by how much information he was able to provide about the miniature sub. When she mentioned the photos that had been taken of the underside of the *Wild Pony* and the strange parallel rows of eight triangular spots, she could hear Joe and Captain Ken talking excitedly in the background.

"Ms. Milagros, my paralegal and I are absolutely certain that we observed eight legs, divided into two rows of four each on the sub in Southampton. And each of the legs had a pie-shaped cup on the end, about the size of a dinner plate. The cups allowed the sub to magnetically attach itself to the bottom of *Crazy Horse*. Ken thinks the legs were spaced about two feet apart. Unfortunately, we were not allowed to take any photos. I just looked at the underwater photo you e-mailed me and we are both pretty certain that the pattern on the bottom of the *Wild Pony* fits the legs that were on the Pilot Fish in Southampton."

"Excuse me?" said Christine. "Pilot Fish?"

"Sorry," said Joe. "That was a code word we were asked to use by our client for the project. Seemed like an apt one to me."

"I agree. Catchy. Now, if only we can catch that sub."

"Ma'am, if you will allow me. The sub was much larger than needed to carry drugs and money. I think it was designed to bring a very large bomb, or bombs to the U.S. It also had a trap door built into the cargo floor, which I believe was intended to drop something to the bottom of the sea. Both Ken and I seriously believe that this silent and sophisticated sub is on its way to Norfolk or New York, or both, to deposit a bomb or bombs in the harbor."

"Seems a bit far-fetched, counselor."

"Perhaps. But you haven't detected the sub so far. Its stealth is worthy of the best American engineers."

"Alright, let's say it was built to carry a bomb. Not much damage a bomb will do if dropped to a riverbed, even in Norfolk or New York. The water will absorb most of the explosion, especially when you consider the depth of those two harbors."

Joe cautiously responded, "Unless the bomb is nuclear. Then, the water would vaporize and the impact, as well as the fallout, would be catastrophic."

"Nuclear? Are you kidding?" responded the Master Chief Petty Officer.

"Wish I were, Ma'am, but the fact is that, given the tension with the North Koreans, and the threats that have been exchanged, as well as the recent rocket launches and nuclear tests, it would be a brilliant idea if the North Koreans sneaked their bombs into the U.S. underwater, while everyone thinks that North Korea has now agreed to dismantle its nuclear weapons research and destroy the missile sites. While everyone is checking the skies, the bombs come in under the sea. More importantly, the explosion goes off and no one knows who did it. North Korea avoids the risk of retaliation and the Chairman gets exactly what he wants – revenge, but no retribution."

Christine was silent for a moment, and then responded in a firm voice, "I have to talk to the higher authorities about this right away. Would you be willing to come to Washington, D.C. to discuss what you have told me?"

"Of course," responded Joe. "But, in the meantime, I would let the container ship *Wild Pony* get back to sea so that she presumably picks up her Pilot Fish again. I am sure that the sub is waiting to rejoin the cargo ship and stayed at sea for fear that there was not enough clearance in the river. Follow her to Norfolk and then stop the ship. Hopefully, you will catch the submarine as well. You got plenty of naval ships to help there."

"Thank you Mr. Barrett. We expect to see you and Mr. Libby tomorrow morning at ten hundred hours in the D.C. office.

"We will be there. However, I suggest you also invite Yeoman Fox from the British Embassy. She knows more than we do about this submarine. Oh, and Ms. Milagros, one other thing. I am looking at my diary on my desk. Thanksgiving is in four days. I have a feeling that is not coincidental."

"Thank you. We will contact their embassy. See you tomorrow, Mr. Barrett."

Chapter 34
Atlantic Ocean

Jian spotted the *Wild Pony* through the sub's periscope as she came out of the Savannah River and followed the buoys out to sea. As the ship dropped off her pilot to the waiting boat, the sub moved silently underneath the idle container ship and quietly attached herself, this time about midship near the keel. Bae efficiently operated all the equipment needed to magnetically attach their vessel. The charts were already up on one of the screens. The distance was approximately 480.4 nautical miles to Norfolk. It was just a matter of simply following the American coastline. Jian was feeling excited about finally getting to perform his role as a hero of his people by laying a bomb in that harbor. It would destroy a large percentage of the American naval fleet, including two aircraft carriers. Hopefully, the fallout would be felt in the American capital as well, which was less than two hundred miles away.

The next twenty-one hours was just a matter of waiting. Jian reviewed the manuals once more for arming the bombs. Each bomb, once dropped to the seabed, was on a special timer that would ensure it would go off at exactly the same time as the other bomb: 12:01 p.m. on November 25, eastern standard time. Each bomb was equipped with a small floating antenna that unwound from the base of the bomb and drifted to the surface. The antennae would allow the devices to communicate with each other over an encrypted signal relayed by Chinese satellites.

Chapter 34

The timing of the explosions was critical. North Korean intelligence revealed that the largest crowds would be outside their homes and buildings at noontime, and thus, exposed to the blast. It was a day the Americans called Thanksgiving, a day, Jian was told, when the Americans celebrated their wealth, privileges, and depravity by drinking and eating too much so as to mock the rest of the world that struggled to put a small meal on the table. He shook his head in disgust as he recalled how his instructors explained that the Americans also put on a huge military parade in New York City that same day. Thousands of people marched down the main street carrying giant statues of their heroes while uniformed bands played provocative marches. Even the children would be there to wave at their heroes and mock the enemies. At the end of the parade, the supreme commander of the armed forces would ride into town on a carriage, surrounded by the spoils of imperialist war, and wearing red to prove that American warriors had spilled blood.

Well, that would all end soon enough. Jian opened a bottle of water and took a sip before turning to Bae, who was reading a book. "Bae, I should think you, always speaking of peace, would be happy to destroy the Americans at their military parade that mocks our leaders and celebrates blood on the battlefield."

Bae looked up from his book, and cautiously replied, "The military parade you speak of is not a military parade. It is a parade for children and is to celebrate the coming of Christmas."

"How do you know this? That is not what we have been told by our instructors."

"Because I was able to get some access to the internet last year and saw news reports and videos of American life."

"That was propaganda. That is why our Leader has prevented such filth from coming into our country." Jian spat in disgust.

"The statutes you speak of are only balloons of children's fairy tales, and the man in red is Santa Clause who is surrounded by toys, not weapons. We are the ones that are being fooled, Jian, not the Americans."

Jian walked angrily back to his berth. "I don't believe it. You are a fool to accept the enemy's propaganda. I may have to report you when we get back."

Without looking up from his book, Bae simply commented, "Jian, do you really think we are going to return home? Do you think we are going to leave two atomic bombs in American cities and we will just steer a route back to our country? No, my friend, this is a one-way trip. I will never see my family again, and you will never see any medals. Even if we survive the nuclear blasts, we will be blown out of the water by their Navy."

Jian raised his voice and shouted, "All of this has been thoroughly planned. We will be back in our homeland in three weeks."

Bae shook his head. "Even if we did make it back to our country, there will be nothing left of it because we – you and I – started a huge war. I believe we won't even make it back to the Panama Canal. Our Leader is very foolish."

This last comment enraged Jian, who picked up a can of tuna fish and threw it at the other man. Bae easily ducked and the tin can crashed into the wall. Jian threw himself into his hammock. He tossed and turned for hours, unable to get any sleep.

In the morning, the men changed shifts and Bae went quietly to his hammock. About three hours later, he was roused by Jian who pushed his shoulder. "Bae, get up. There is a problem. The *Wild Pony* is slowing down and we still have two hours to go before we reach the pick-up point for the Norfolk pilot. Get on the instruments and see what you can hear."

Chapter 34

Bae went straight to the controls. He read the instruments and put on a headset. After a couple of minutes, it was clear there was a worried look on his face. "Jian, there are several vessels approaching us at high speed. At least one naval ship, I think it is one of the new LCS frigates. There are also some boats with several outboard engines on each – probably Coast Guard Defender class. There are some slower but larger vessels following in the distance, perhaps a cutter. I fear we have been discovered."

"Not yet, we haven't. Quick, disengage the magnetic arms attached to the freighter." With a determined face, Jian checked the charts and quickly pressed the controls to ballast the sub."

"Done. Shall I start the magneto engines?" asked Bae.

"No. first, let's sink to the bottom. The sea is over a hundred eighty meters in depth here and the bottom is made of soft mud. Let the container ship continue moving forward. When they stop her, they will probably send over divers. Hopefully, we will be far enough away and buried in the mud so that they cannot detect us. The sound insulation on the outside surface of our sub should be enough to prevent any reflection of their underwater sonar signals. After that, all we need do is wait till they leave and then head directly for New York." Another four minutes passed. Bae looked up at the overhead monitor. "The *Wild Pony* has stopped her engines, but I think, due to inertia, she will continue to drift forward for about a half kilometer." He again listened to his headset and looked at the numbers on the screen. "One, no two, of the naval ships are turning to follow the cargo ship. They may not know that we have released our grip on the ship."

Jian looked at the overhead monitor, which showed a wire-mesh schemata of the ocean bottom. It was uneven, with an undulating surface. This would help disguise the sub once it landed in the mud. "Eighteen more meters and we are on the bottom. We have to slow our descent so as not to make any accidental noise." He quickly made some adjustments on the keypad. A few seconds later, the submarine stopped as it was sucked into the ocean bed.

Chapter 35
Territorial Waters

The two Navy divers were over the sides of the rigid bottom inflatable the moment the container ship slowed to less than three knots. Any faster than that and the divers would have trouble keeping up with the vessel. Both divers held high-powered underwater lights rated at over a million candlepower each. They helped cut through the dark ocean water with streaks of white light, but after little more than fifty feet, the bright lights were absorbed into the murk and inky darkness. The beams of light swung back and forth over the bottom of the ship. The headgear of both divers took continuous video of what was in front of them. The video was transmitted to the tri-hull Littoral Combat Ship (LCS), *USS Independence*, which was positioned about one hundred yards away. Its futuristic, sleek shape allowed for speeds in excess of forty knots. A thirty-millimeter Gatling gun manufactured by Teledyne Brown Engineering was aimed at the bridge of the *Wild Pony*. At two hundred fifty rounds a minute, it would obliterate the wheel house of the *Wild Pony* in a matter of two minutes. The Navy ship was also towing a Thales anti-submarine module, which was developed to detect diesel-electric submarines.

Both Master Chief Petty Officer Milagros and Yeoman Fox were in the tactical warfare room of the combat ship looking at several large video images of the container ship on the wall, as well as the underwater videos being transmitted by the divers. Another monitor showed the ship from overhead by a camera mounted on a flying drone. It was clear there was no submarine attached to the bottom of the container ship, but fresh scrapings of bottom paint near the centerline of the ship indicated the Pilot Fish had been there. The pattern of two rows of four dish-shaped chips in the surface paint were identical to the other scrapings only fifty feet further aft, but were not in the photos taken at Savannah.

"Damn, we missed it again," said Christine, staring hard at the videos. "And tactical just reported that nothing was heard on the sonar array, although there was a momentary recording of something in the order of a light thump. Not sure what that was. I am afraid that our electronics are not going to be able to detect the magneto drive. Maybe we will get lucky with one of the underwater hydrophones along the East Coast."

Yeoman Fox was looking at some printouts of the engineering reports from the scientists in the U.K. regarding the testing of the engines. "I agree, it will be very difficult to locate the sub through traditional sonar. The only way I can see us finding the sub now is with a ferrous metal detector. Some of the new detectors are sensitive to less than one nanotesla."

Master Chief Petty officer Milagros looked incredulous. "You mean we use a metal detector, like the ones that kids use on the beach to find coins?"

"Well, a bit more sophisticated than that, of course. But yes, the electrical generator on the sub needed to produce the energy to operate the magneto drive is highly ferrous and dense, even if compact. We have been developing a unit to tow underwater for a couple of years that will detect even very slight indications of ferrous materials. Still experimental, but it may work. Let me contact my government and see if we can get one delivered to this ship."

"But what do we do for now?' asked Milagros.

CHAPTER 35

"My suggestion is that you don't let the *Wild Pony* into Norfolk. Too many naval ships there, and a bit too close to Washington, if I am correct." Fox thought for a moment. "On the other hand, maybe you should let the ship continue to New York – that's her final port of call in the U.S., right?"

"Yes. But why would we do that?"

"Because the pilot of the sub may be anxious enough not to want to go into any port without some cover. He could look for another vessel to latch onto, but he would have to wait until the right one came by. However, the sub requires the freighter to slow down enough to perform the attachment procedure. It won't happen out here in the open sea; however, if we let the *Wild Pony* go on to New York, the pilot of the sub may decide that she has been checked by your Navy and found clean, so it is doubtful anyone would come back." She paused. "As the expression goes, the better the devil you know than the one you don't. And before the *Wild Pony* arrives in New York, hopefully we can come up with a plan to better track the sub underwater. I should have the new ferrous detector in place by then."

Christine saw a lot of gaps in the strategy, but also knew there was no better plan. Between Homeland Security, the FBI, the Coast Guard, and the Navy weighing in on this situation, she would have to run it up the flag pole. "OK, let me see what can be done."

Christine picked up her phone and dialed her Commander. Five minutes later, he was on the phone with Homeland Security in Washington. Everyone was taking a chance of letting the fox into the hen house if Christine's plan failed. A half-hour later, Christine got the word to let the container ship go. She apologized to the captain of the *Wild Pony* in order to play up the mistake, in case he was in touch with the submarine. However, she passed on the order to the Captain of the LCS to keep the sonar going and the drones flying. The *Independence* was to shadow the container ship from just over the horizon distance so that the *Wild Pony* would not know it was being followed.

Nearly six hundred feet below, in the icy Atlantic water, Jian and Bae sat rigid in the command chairs, fearful of making any sound that could be heard by the warships above. Jian kept looking at the monitors, which showed the sounds of the engines from the various ships above. They could not use active sonar as the ping would be heard by everyone on the surface. Jian was rapidly thinking of the remaining options. They could move underwater all the way to New York harbor, but he knew there were a lot of secret underwater sound buoys along the American coastline. Even if the buoys were unable to detect their virtually silent engines, there was the issue of whether the American underwater receivers were sensitive enough to pick up the sound of the water moving around their hull. He could not risk rising to the surface or having an antennae float above water, as any transmission would probably be picked up not only by the Navy but also by American satellites and shore facilities. With some triangulation, they would be able to pinpoint exactly where the transmission was coming from, even if it was not decrypted. Jian had to make the decision on his own. This was a contingency that had not been anticipated by his superiors.

Bae continued staring at the monitors. "Jian, the naval boats are beginning to move away and pick up speed. They are heading back towards Norfolk."

"And what about the *Wild Pony*?"

"It looks like she is slowly turning, but towards sea! Yes, she is also increasing rpms, and headed north."

Jian grinned. "So, your fears of the great American military might are wrong. They did not find anything and they have gone home. They must be very embarrassed."

"Still, the container ship is no longer on a course into Norfolk. Why? Something has happened. I do not think it safe to go back to riding under the container ship. We can reach New York on our own and find another ship waiting to enter the port."

"Why?" said Jian, with more than a bit of overconfidence. "The American Navy has checked the *Wild Pony*, and they know that we are not under that ship. They will now have to start looking elsewhere. What better place to hide than under the ship they have already inspected?" He could be heard chuckling. "Let's head for the container ship now before she is going too fast for us to latch on to her."

Bae looked at Jian with amazement. Did his commanding officer really think that having gone this far in finding evidence of the sub that the Americans would stop because there was nothing seen under the *Wild Pony?* The Americans obviously suspected something when they sent five ships out to intercept the Korean container ship. For Bae, this was a bad sign that their plans had been discovered. It was just a matter of time till their sub was caught.

Jian knew the look on his friend's face. He did not want to appear cocky or undisciplined. "Once we get under the ship, let's keep a close ear for anything nearby. If the Navy is following us, then we can drop off this freighter and do the task on our own."

Chapter 36
East River

"Promise me you won't peek?" Joe asked, with a hint of humor in his voice.

"Joe, you have my head wrapped up in this scarf tighter than a mummy. I better not fall!" Dalia responded as she gingerly felt with her feet whether there was solid ground in front of her. "I don't know how you talked me into this." She lifted her elbow to indicate there was a step in front of her.

"All I did was ask. Sweetly, I might add. You agreed. Now you have to do your part. I assure you it will be worthwhile."

Dalia had no idea where they were. Joe had driven in circles while she was blindfolded. They were definitely outdoors, and she could hear a seagull or two, so she figured they must be near the water. Indeed, as she cocked her head to one side, she could hear water lapping up against a wall. But instead of a fresh sea breeze, there was a slight mechanical odor that she could not place and a thumping sound that seemed to come from underground.

"One more high step, and then two steps down. And voilà, we have arrived," joked Joe. He was obviously enjoying himself.

The last step was an unexpected one. It was onto a metal surface and the surface was moving; slowly, but definitely shifting both up and down and left and right. Joe reached behind her head, loosened the blindfold, and let it drop from her face. The slight wind immediately caught the silk scarf and whisked it up in the air, and then it paused momentarily over her head and was suddenly blown away by another puff. After drifting a dozen yards, it gently settled into the mirror-like black water.

Joe kissed Dalia fully on the lips before she could determine where they were. As he pulled his head back, she realized they were on a boat. A quick scan and it was clear that it was not just any boat but an old tug boat; the greasy kind, with just a hint of a smell of machine oil.

"Well, I don't know what to say. Must admit, I have never had a man shanghai me onto a tugboat in the middle of the night."

"Was kind of betting on that, but give me a chance. This will be worth it." Joe looked up to the tug's wheelhouse. An elderly bald man with a Van Dyke beard looked out the port window and smiled. The engines coughed and a thrush of white water appeared off the stern. The huge tug slowly moved away from the seawall and headed down the East River. Dalia finally got her bearings and realized that they had stepped into the boat from a landing for pilots and police boats near 61st Street and the FDR Drive.

"Ah, Joe, give me a hint. Where are we going? And I must say that you are very lucky it turned out relatively warm tonight; otherwise, I would be hiding below in the engine room."

Joe put his jacket around her, and then his arm around her waist. He walked her to the platform at the rear of the tugboat. They watched the wake slowly drift into the distance as the Queensboro Bridge and the tall city buildings sent little pinpricks of colored lights onto the water's dark surface. *Admittedly, it's beautiful*, Dalia thought.

"Perhaps I should explain," Joe said.

"Good start," replied Dalia with a half-amused, half-quizzical look on her face.

"Well, the tug is named the *Ms. Charlotte* and I have known its owner, Frank, for many years. In college, I needed a job. Money was tight. I had a friend at school who suggested I talk to Frank. He hired me on the spot, even though the only boat I had ever been on was the Staten Island Ferry. I learned a lot that summer, and he was kind enough to hire me back every summer through law school. My love of the sea is, in large part, due to Frank taking a gamble on me."

Joe looked up along the shoreline. "The city has changed, but riding on the river is always the same. You follow its path."

Joe scanned the water around them. "Isn't it beautiful how calm the water can get?"

Dalia studied Joe's face. "But Joe, you still haven't told me why we are here."

"Frank was kind enough to loan me his tug tonight. I needed this open space, the stars overhead, and the city lights for this important moment." Joe held Dalia close with her head in his hands. "Dalia, I want you to travel with me on the same path forever. When I look into my heart, all I see is you."

He fell to his knee and reached into the right pocket of his pants. There was a sudden look of panic on his face and he shifted so as to reach into his left pocket. He smiled and pulled out a small, black velvet box. He slowly opened it. Dalia was amazed by how, even in the pitch dark of the night, the stars and shore lights all merged in the center stone of the beautiful diamond ring.

Joe said quietly, "Will you marry me?"

"It's beautiful, Joe." She wiped tears from her eyes and then stared at him. "I really did not expect this. You caught me by utter surprise... I love you." She reached out and passionately kissed him.

When their lips pulled apart, Joe pulled his head back and commented, "I am assuming that was a yes?"

Chapter 36

Dalia smiled and shook her head affirmatively as she wiped a tear from her cheek. Joe looked up at the wheelhouse and nodded. The tug's huge horns blasted several times to the point where Dalia had to cover her ears. Barrett laughed and held her tight. They watched as the Statue of Liberty came into view and the white lights of downtown Manhattan surrounded them. Then, the tug slowly swung around and headed leisurely back to the seawall.

Chapter 37
Atlantic Ocean

Master Chief Petty Officer Milagros quickly scanned the reports as she stood in the command center of the LCS *Independence*, which was monitoring the *Wild Pony* as it steamed about twenty miles ahead. Since they were in the commercial northbound traffic lane along the East Coast, it would be doubtful that the container ship would become suspicious that there was a vessel following behind. Indeed, from what Christine could see on the plotting chart, there were at least a dozen large commercial vessels in the same area, all heading north towards New York and Boston.

Homeland Security had given the rogue submarine high priority since the investigation in Savannah. Christine Milagros looked around the command center in the heart of the vessel's superstructure. It was hard not to be impressed by the state of the art equipment that was crammed into the large room, and the professional caliber of the sailors working around her. Low red lighting from the ceiling and walls gave the windowless room the feeling of something out of a science fiction movie. Technicians manned dozens of desks, where they monitored electronic information and communications that were continuously sent and received by the sensitive towers above the bridge house. A wall-sized monitor was situated in the middle of the room displaying telescopic and satellite images of the *Wild Pony*, as well as her positioning on marine charts.

Chapter 37

So far, the advanced electronics on the warship had not been able to detect any craft attached to the bottom of the *Wild Pony*, nor had the secret sound sensors hidden in the bottom of the ocean along the East Coast. The fact was that commercial ships in coastal waters generated a lot of noise in the 10 kHz to 40 kHz range. The Navy had been compiling a huge library of the sounds made by every major vessel known, which focused mostly on the pitch and resonance of the propellers as they turned in the water. The sounds of the tiny air bubbles created by cavitation around the blades could be heard by the sensitive microphones.

The technical staff on the *Independence* said that the computers identified and confirmed most of the sounds from the *Wild Pony*, which had been secretly recorded soon after the container ship was launched. The only odd thing noted by the staff was that the sounds measured from sensors located forward of the ship seemed to be a bit muted compared to sounds measured from all other angles around the ship. One tech suggested this might be caused by a sub attached to the bottom of the *Wild Pony*, which was blocking, or at least interfering, with sound waves traveling forward from the propellers. However, no one could be certain. Christine realized that the only proof that everyone would accept would be visual proof of, as the New York lawyer dubbed it, the "Pilot Fish." However, even a U.S. Naval sub submerged underwater did not have windows to allow it to peer under the bottom of the container ship. The best bet would be to launch a robot sub, or drone, to monitor the container ship on its way to New York. A drone could get under the cargo ship and use its sensitive video cameras to transmit images directly to the warship. Indeed, if they did it right, they could use the drone to plant a tracker bug on the outside skin of the sub. That would allow them to follow the Pilot Fish, even if it suddenly went off on its own.

Christine turned to the other tech working at her table. "How's the robot fish coming along?"

"Ready to go, Ma'am. She can do almost forty knots underwater, so it will be able to catch up quickly with the *Wild Pony*. We have ideal conditions for its operation."

"Good. I want it in the water and within a hundred yards of the container ship before she arrives at the pilot station off Sandy Hook. The *Wild Pony* will have to slow down for the harbor pilot to come on board. I want the drone taking lots of pictures the moment her speed is decreased. And if that sub is there, get it tagged."

"Yes, Ma'am. We'll let you know when the drone is five minutes out from the target." The seaman went back to his computer completing the instructions that would be downloaded into the drone's onboard computer. The robot, only eight feet long and less than a foot in diameter, looked more like a torpedo than a mini-sub. It was already prepped and sitting in a launcher tube on the port side. Two minutes later, it blasted out of the tube, followed by a puff of white smoke. It landed in the water with hardly a splash. A white streak on the surface of the sea was the only evidence that it was speeding towards its target. Soon, even the white bubbles disappeared as the drone reached a depth of twenty feet. Its track was shown as a blinking red dot on the command board – and it was quickly catching up with the green triangle, which was the position of the *Wild Pony*. Now all that could be done was wait.

* * *

Onboard the Pilot Fish, Jian kept turning the pages as he closely re-read the instructions on initiating the countdown for the bombs, and then how to drop them through the hatch to the bottom of the harbor. The instructions were clear enough, but one fact that Jian only realized now was that once the bombs were initiated, it was difficult to shut them off. He had memorized the shut-off code back at the naval academy. There was to be no copy of that code aboard the sub. Maybe Bae was right; their superiors knew this was a one-way ride and that the two submariners would not be coming back.

His faith that the bombs would not explode the moment they were dropped from the bay doors was that his superiors said they had gone to great pains to link the two bombs together so that they would go off simultaneously. The Chairman wanted the United States and the rest of the world to know that it was not some terrorist plot, but rather a well-planned attack that could only be organized under the control of a nation with sophisticated and advanced technology. With the assistance of a Chinese satellite, the controllers in Pyongyang would be able to link the two bombs to ensure they went off simultaneously. Of course, the Chairman wanted the explosion to be at the end of the Macy's Thanksgiving day parade when millions would be lining the streets of Manhattan. Jian had been told that the best place to position the bomb in New York would be in the East River near the United Nations building. Not only would the blast roar up 34th Street into the waving hands of the military leader in the red suit but it would also take down the U.N. building. The coordinated efforts by the members of the U.N. to strangle their country had left the Chairman angry and vengeful. He would now pay them back in full for having tightened the leash to the point where his country was gasping its last breath. No one would challenge North Korea again.

"Jian, come here. I think we have a problem," said Bae.
"What is it?"

"The sound sensors have picked up a very fast and small vessel coming towards us from the South."

"Can you identify what it is?" Jian asked.

"No. It is surprisingly hard to hear and there is interference from the propellers of the container ship on top of us. Our sensors are not getting a full bearing on the object and the sound graph does not match anything in our computer base.

"How long before it arrives?" "Maybe five minutes."

Jian could not raise the periscope without detaching the sub from the Wild Pony and drifting away. But then they would lose the cover of the container ship.

"Can you tell if it is military or just some speedboat? Maybe it's one of those Jetski craft?"

"I cannot tell you. Our equipment does not identify it. All I know is that it is very small. It is not a navy or coast guard ship. By the way, the *Wild Pony* has started to slow down. We must be near the position where the harbor pilot comes on board to steer the ship into New York harbor."

Jian was very quiet as he thought about their options. "Maybe this is a good time to go in alone. I think we have overstayed our welcome with the *Wild Pony*. Arrange to disconnect."

Bae looked at his friend and senior officer. He hoped Jian was right. This was not the plan. With that, Bae went through the steps on his computer screen to power off the electromagnets on each of the eight legs, and mechanically fold them into the side of the sub's hull. There was a sense of panic when the seventh leg would not dislodge. Perhaps it had wedged itself into some crack in the hull plating of the container ship. After the third try, the leg finally broke free, although it would not fully fold into its travel position.

"We have another problem, Jian. The seventh attachment leg is broken. I managed to clear it from the hull of the container ship, but it won't fold into place. We may not be able to reattach ourselves to another ship if the alignment of the legs is now off."

CHAPTER 37

"What else can go wrong? Bring us up to five meters so that I can raise the periscope. Let's see where we are and how we get into the harbor."

Bae adjusted the angle of the sub and brought it slowly up to periscope depth. The periscope was actually a small video camera the size of a thin, pencil-width rod that lifted just above the water's edge. The live feed from the camera was projected onto the video screen at the front of the sub. Jian's first reaction was to blink with the brightness from the sunlit scene. They had not seen sunlight in weeks. The water was choppy, but no significant waves. Jian and Bae could see the Verrazano Bridge in the distance connecting Brooklyn and Staten Island, and to the east of that was the tall Ferris wheel and parachute jump at Coney Island. Swinging the joystick, they could see the beaches around Sandy Hook in New Jersey.

There was a lot of marine traffic. Two huge container ships, about the same size as the *Wild Pony*, were coming out of New York harbor and had just passed under the bridge. Several tanker vessels were anchored along the Brooklyn shoreline. At least two blue-colored, high-speed ferries could be seen hugging the coastline heading towards the bridge. Several fishing vessels were traveling single file out towards the south shore of Long Island, and a scow used to transport garbage was headed into the city.

"Where is that small high-speed craft you were talking about?"

"It's not showing up on the software. I don't know where it is."

"There are some high-speed ferries out here. Maybe that's what the computer was hearing."

Bae assumed there was no use arguing with his boss. The sound was certainly not from a ferry. But now that he could not identify the object, and there was only silence, fighting with Jian over the importance of the object would serve no purpose.

"Maybe," he responded.

"I think I have found us cover into the harbor. There is a large garbage scow about four hundred meters off of our starboard bow. Can you pinpoint it? Good, let's see if we can get underneath the scow. As I remember the training materials, the scow travels daily up the East River, right by the United Nations and then continues onto someplace called Astoria. It's big, it's loud, and it does not draw much depth because it has a flat bottom. It should be perfect."

"Bae, you probably should turn on the VHF radio intercepts. If they are after us, it will be on the marine radio."

* * *

Christine Milagros was watching her own wall-size monitor with a half-dozen other officers and technicians. The underwater picture taken from the nose camera on the drone was dark and murky, but thank God there was enough sunlight filtering through the sea to provide visibility for about fifty feet. The drone slowed down as it approached the stern of the *Wild Pony*. The view from the drone's camera showed the transom of the container ship with the name in ten-foot-high white lettering. They had the right target.

The driver of the drone sat in a huge black leather chair facing the center of the screen. He used his right hand to gently manipulate the joystick, which was positioned on a mechanical arm in front of him. The screen showed critical information along the edge of the picture: the drone's depth, GPS coordinates, water temperature, heading, and signal reception. Another insert at the bottom of the screen showed a nautical chart of New York with both the positions of both the drone and the target. Vector lines from the target indicated its presumed path.

Chapter 37

The driver carefully maneuvered the water drone around the side of the vessel to avoid the wash of the two giant bronze propellers that were turning slowly. The periscope revealed that the pilot boat had already come alongside the container vessel. The turbulence created by the props made it difficult to see anything clearly from the underwater camera until the drone moved past the vessel's stern. The foamy white bubbles in the water quickly disappeared and a clear view of the massive bottom of the *Wild Pony* was displayed on the monitor. There was no sub attached. However, everyone's eyes were riveted to the right-hand side of the screen. There was a thin tubular white wake, like a long wispy puff of smoke, which trailed from under the ship to the right side of the huge monitor before disappearing off the screen. The white ribbon slowly dissolved in the darkness of the ocean.

"Follow that wake. Try to catch up," Christine ordered the Robotics Warfare Specialist controlling the drone. Immediately, a sense of added speed could be seen in the water as tiny bubbles sped by the nose camera.

"Do we have a lock on the object?" Christine inquired.

"No Ma'am, there is no sound from turning screws. The hydro-magnetic drive is impossible to trace."

Christine looked up at Yeoman Fox. "Did your package from the U.K. arrive? We could really use it about now."

Fox smiled back. "Already assembled and ready to drop over the side. The ferrous detector should pick it up within minutes." Fox immediately spoke into the com mounted over her ear.

The Chief Petty Officer spoke to the technician at the table to her left. "Meanwhile, keep tracking any sound of cavitation on the sub's hull as it moves through the water. It can't avoid making some bubbles."

Meanwhile, Yeoman Fox was working at another computer station with a young technician who was typing furiously at his keyboard. Fox looked up and smiled. "I think we got a fix. Put it up on the master monitor." Everyone stared at the wall. The huge control room monitor flickered, and then the screen was divided into two. The new screen to the right was a mesh graph. A red dot in the shape of a delta came into view on the graph. Above the dot was information concerning speed, distance, and direction. The red symbol flickered in and out several times. Again, the officer spoke. "The contact is a bit spotty, probably due to layers of various temperatures in the water, salinity, floating particles and abandoned iron objects on the bottom of the ocean. But it looks like our target is about a hundred yards in front of our drone. Heading 015 degrees at a speed of about 20 knots."

Christine was puzzled as she looked at the chart of New York harbor in front of her. "Where's he going, folks? It's not the shortest route to the Verrazano Bridge. He seems to be angled off towards the Brooklyn shoreline." There was a long pause as everyone studied the information on their screens.

The tech was the first to speak. "I think the sub is trying to intersect with a vessel that is headed into New York Harbor. Let me check its electronic identification. It's a garbage scow!" Others looked up and nodded in agreement.

"Get me the name and details of that scow. And get me the cell phone of the captain. I don't want to call on the VHF since the sub could be listening." Several phones were immediately picked up and computer screens at various stations ran through different views. Within three minutes, Milagros was on the ship's sat phone talking with Captain Derrick James of the scow *Manhattan*. The scow was one of three vessels designed to transport semi-solid materials from an aeration facility in Queens. Each day, the scows were filled with processed waste material and navigated to a facility near JFK airport where the waste was ultimately turned into processed landfill. The scow was now returning empty.

"Captain James, This is Master Chief Petty Officer Christine Milagros of the U.S. Coast Guard. We are tracking a potentially dangerous enemy submarine, which is currently headed underwater towards New York Harbor. We have tracked its path towards your vessel. We suspect it intends to hide under your ship while you travel up the harbor."

There was a pause and some static on the phone before the rough and bass voice of Captain James responded, "Lady, is this a joke? An enemy submarine in New York Harbor?"

"This is no joke, sir. You are welcome to call my superior officer in Washington D.C., Admiral Deerfield, and he will confirm how serious I am. This is his number. Call it and then call me back as soon as possible."

"Alright lady, but if this is a joke, I am going to report you to the Coast Guard."

"Sir, it's not a joke, you have a bomb sitting underneath your ship. And I am the Coast Guard!"

Three minutes later, the scow captain called back. "OK, you have my attention. What can I do?"

"Where are you headed?"

"The city waste facility on Newton Creek. Do you know it?"

"I have it on my screen. The mini-sub is about one hundred yards off your port side at a depth of thirty feet. How much does your vessel draw?"

"About twelve feet. We are empty."

"Please proceed at your current speed and route. We don't want the sub to suspect it's been located. What is your expected ETA in the Kips Bay area before you turn into the Creek?"

"Probably ten a.m. Seems to me that it would make more sense for me to circle around and head back out to sea."

"The sub will just look for another mother ship to hide under, or worse, go it alone. Better that we know where it is."

"Easy for you to say. You're not sitting on top of a bomb," responded the captain, who was obviously not happy about being used as bait. "So, what's the plan, lady? I don't think it is going to follow me up into Newtown Creek. Too shallow. Where is it headed, by the way?"

Milagros looked at the staff around her. It was a good question. She didn't know where the sub was going to drop the bomb in the harbor – in front of the Statue of Liberty, in the river at the end of Wall Street, or perhaps under the Brooklyn Bridge. Her whole strategy was based upon the assumption that the sub would give itself enough time to leave New York Harbor and get far enough away before detonating the bomb. That would probably take at least an hour or two.

"Lady, can you hear me? What's the plan? I was supposed to pick my wife and kids up after the Thanksgiving Day parade. I've got to let them know if I'm going to be late."

Christine's eyes widened. That was it: the Thanksgiving Day parade. If the bomb went off in the East River near 34th Street, where the parade ended, millions of visitors would be wiped out. Christine held her hand over the mouthpiece and said to the group, "What if he's planning on setting the bomb off in the river near 34th Street? The Thanksgiving Day Parade is on today."

"Just started Ma'am. It should end about noon."

One of the techs at the computers looked up and commented, "That's also a couple of blocks from where the United Nations is located."

"Should we get the patrol boats up there?" The Coast Guard unit in New York had several rigid hull inflatable craft that were very fast, with three engines putting out nearly one thousand horsepower. The craft were equipped with fifty-caliber machine guns in the bow. They were often used to provide security in the river when there were special events at the United Nations. New York City also operated a couple of serious tactical patrol boats as well.

"If the sub sees the patrol craft coming, I am concerned they will trigger an explosion without leaving the harbor first. If we are quiet, and they drop the bomb to the bottom of the river, we have a chance of finding it with the ferrous detector tracer while they try to escape." Christine thought for a moment. "We need to talk to Barrett, that maritime lawyer in New York. He's seen the inside of the sub. Can they just drop the bomb out of the sub while it is moving, or do they have to stop the sub and then lower the bomb to the seabed? Does the sub have to sit on the bottom to plant the bomb?" As she scrolled through her phone, she spoke to the communication tech sitting at the desk in front of her. "Here's his number. Joe Barrett. Call him. Quick."

A few seconds later, the phone could be heard ringing over the speaker system.

"Joe Barrett. May I help you?"

"Joe, this is Master Petty Chief Officer Christine Milagros. You called me about the mystery sub you referred to as the Pilot Fish. Do you recall?"

"Yes Ma'am. I remember. How can I help?"

"We tracked the sub. It's entering New York Harbor as we speak. I am on a naval vessel following it. Far as we can figure, it is headed up the East River and will probably try to plant the bomb in the river off 34th Street."

"Holy shit," Joe gasped. Controlling himself, he spoke again. "Sorry about that. What can I do to help?"

"You went inside the other mini-sub in the U.K., right? I need to know right now how the sub drops the bomb in the harbor. Is there a hatch? Is there equipment to lower the bomb to the bottom? Can the hatch be opened while the sub is moving? We need an idea of how long it is going to take them to get it in place."

As she was talking, Joe texted Dalia:

Get the hell out of town. Grab your family and drive as far away as possible. Bomb coming into NY Harbor!

"Mr. Barrett, are you listening?" asked Christine.

"Yes, I am trying to visually remember what I saw. There was a trap door in the center of the cargo room. About fifteen feet long. Floor went down, not up. It was all controlled from the pilot station. There were no winches, straps, or wires in the sub I was on. I assume the doors were on hinges and simply lowered down, letting the bombs fall to the bottom of the ocean, or river. Probably means the sub needs to sit still just above the river bottom to accurately place the bomb, otherwise the bombs could tumble on the riverbed if they were dropped from a greater height."

"Thank you, Mr. Barrett, that's what I needed to know. Hopefully that means the sub will give itself at least a couple of hours after planting the bombs while it tries to escape New York Harbor."

"Good point. If it's not a suicide mission. But there is something you ought…"

He heard a click and the phone went dead. He had not been able to tell her that there was a way to stop the sub. He tried calling back, but the Chief Petty Officer's phone just rang and rang.

Chapter 38
Port of New York

Bae sat in the huge swivel chair listening intently through his headset, watching the information flowing across the big flat screen. As he slowly turned a dial, he looked over at Jian.

"Still no indication on the VHF channels or any alerts about spotting a sub."

Jian grinned as he continued to manipulate the joystick a degree or two so as to steer the underwater vessel with the scow only thirty feet above them. The deep rumble of the twin propellers thrashing the water over their heads could be felt through the sub's skin.

"Stupid Americans. We are walking into their greatest city carrying nuclear bombs and they know nothing. How naive we were to think they might catch us."

Bae did not respond. The statement ignored all that had happened over the past twenty-four hours. The Americans were out there. It was *they* who did not know the location of the Americans.

"Bae, you have to take control of steering. It's time for me to initiate the arming of the bombs." Jian then got up from the pilot seat and headed back towards the large steel crates behind him. He tapped in the code on the small keypad and opened a panel on the left wall of the first weapon. Although he knew the procedures by heart, having repeated them every day during the voyage, he still held the instructions page in front of him. There was a sudden whir of machinery, and the lights on the panel built into the crate blinked as they went through an initiation sequence. Jian waited for each prompt before entering the additional information required.

Bae looked quickly over his shoulder at his long-time friend and colleague. "Jian, we don't have to do this. We don't have to murder millions of people. This will not make our country great. We will only bring shame to our family names."

"You are wrong, Bae. This will indeed make us heroes, and bring respect to our families. We will be applauded by our Chairman and our families will be well taken care of should anything go wrong."

"Has it occurred to you that the Chairman could just as easily deny that he had anything to do with the bombing and say that it was done by two radical and out-of-control agents whom the government disavows and condemns?"

"Why would he do that?"

Jian frowned and looked over his shoulder. "Because he gets his personal wish to bomb the United States, but at the same time, he avoids the backlash that will come with murdering all these innocent people. Our country cannot take more sanctions, let alone be the focus of a retaliatory war by countries from all over the world. The Chairman will simply say we stole the submarine and he could not find us. He is very sorry."

Jian stopped for a moment before looking down at the bomb's control panel. "No, I don't believe our Chairman would do that. He has made clear that he wants to destroy the criminal American government and its people and demonstrate the superiority and power of North Korea."

Bae sadly responded, "If that is true, my good friend, then why are we sneaking into New York? Why then, will we,—hopefully, sneak out of New York, and why will we set these bombs off with no warning whatsoever? If the bombs were launched on missiles from our country, then the world would know where the bombs came from. I fear these bombs will never be acknowledged."

Jian scowled. The last thing he needed now was to argue politics with his comrade. Rather than respond, he went back to completing the initiation of the first bomb and then started on the second bomb.

"Where are we now?" asked Jian.

"If my instruments are correct, we are coming up on the Williamsburg Bridge. In about twenty minutes, we should enter into Kips Bay.

Thirty-fourth Street is about halfway across that bay."

Jian could see the chart in his head. "When we are near the center of that bay, you will head towards the tall navigation light on Belmont Island. It is on your map. It is a pile of rocks just a few hundred meters south of the tip of Roosevelt Island, right in the middle of the East River. The depth of the water around those rocks is only about six meters. That should be a perfect place for us to drop the bombs. The admiral instructed us to avoid dropping the device in the middle of Kips Bay because the water is very deep and will absorb too much of the explosion.

"But Jian. At six meters, we will be very close to the surface of the water; a part of our vessel could be seen from above the water. Can't we unload the bombs someplace deeper?"

"No. We will put the bombs where our leaders have instructed." Jian sneered for a moment. "Besides, my friend, the shallow island with its rocks will also help focus the explosion towards the United Nations buildings. The admiral told me that the Chairman made it clear he wants the entire United Nations complex destroyed because of their lack of spine and their favoritism towards the United States." Bae kept watching the huge screen in front of his chair. Suddenly, he sat up. "Jian, we may have a problem. I think the barge scow is beginning to turn away from the river. Maybe they have found us!"

Chapter 39
Kips Bay

Joe drove like a maniac down Vernon Boulevard in Astoria. The street was always crowded, and a lot of commercial vehicles used it as a way to avoid going through the heart of the village.

The road wound along the eastern channel of the East River, just across from Roosevelt Island. The three-mile island, inhabited by about fourteen thousand people, sat right in the middle of the East River underneath the Queensboro Bridge. Two massive stone pillars on the southern end of Roosevelt Island acted as supports for the double-decker bridge that crossed from 59th Street in Manhattan to Northern Boulevard in Queens. Alongside the bridge was a red Swiss-built cable car that ran parallel to the bridge and landed in the middle of Roosevelt Island.

As the warehouses in Astoria flashed by, Joe kept his left hand on the horn, blasting the cars in front of him out of the way. He grabbed cell phone from the passenger seat with his right hand, looked down to scroll through his contacts, narrowly missing a green-colored taxicab coming the opposite way. All he could see of the driver side was a large middle-finger aimed in his direction. Joe found the number and hit dial. "Frank, this is the most important request I have made in my life. I need the *Ms. Charlotte* Now. At 44th Drive in Long Island City. Water's edge. Believe me when I say our lives, all our lives, depend upon it." He threw the phone back on the seat and grabbed the steering wheel with both hands to drive blind around a stopped city bus. Horns blasted from every direction.

At the corner of 44th Drive, Joe ignored the red light and threw the wheel over and screeched around the tight bend. Two short blocks and he screeched to a halt in front of the edge of the East River, or more correctly, the defunct restaurant known for many years as Water's Edge. The restaurant was actually a floating barge that had been destroyed by Hurricane Sandy. The building was boarded up, parts of it missing, and the paint was discolored and stained. However, what the dilapidated restaurant had next to it was a beautiful, refurbished concrete and steel pier that jutted at least two-hundred feet out into the East River just off the southern tip of Roosevelt Island. That end of the Island, only about three hundred yards across the river from the end of the pier, was known as Four Freedom's Park, named after the famous speech by Franklin D. Roosevelt. Beautiful landscaped grass and evenly spaced trees narrowed towards the tip of the island, bordered by a sturdy granite and concrete bullhead that gave the park the feeling of being the bow of a warship. Just beyond the very southern tip of the island was a pile of rocks jutting above the water known as Belmont Island. It was no larger than a city bus. A steel tower was mounted in the middle of the island with a green colored navigation light on its top. The only ones attracted to Belmont were seagulls, which used it as a target, and local fishermen, who found porgies and blues plentiful in the rip currents that surrounded the little isle.

Joe threw open the door to his car and ran onto the pier. A few hundred yards south of the pier was a blue and white tug headed in his direction. Mounted under the wheelhouse window was a large steel plate with the name *Ms. Charlotte* written on it. Joe thought the boat was a lot larger in daylight compared to when he and Dalia had taken the moonlight cruise. Captain Frank, with his white beard, was leaning out the window waiving towards Joe, signaling for him to jump on board where the pier ended. When the tug's bow glided in just a foot away from the pier's pylon, Joe took a leap and landed with cat–like precision on the steel deck. Without stopping, he ran to the side door and bounded up the steps to the bridge. Frank had already put the tug into reverse, its engines rumbling as they strained to throw the massive propellers in the opposite direction. Slowly, the tug backed up, black smoke spitting out of the stacks. The bow swung around.

"What's up, Joe? Your message sounded pretty serious."

"Frank, I know you won't believe me, but there is a mini-sub coming up the East River, and I am pretty certain it has at least one nuclear bomb on board, which it intends to explode."

Captain Frank curled his thick eyebrows and his eyes beaded. Joe was not sure he had heard him. Then, Frank looked over at Joe with a slow smile on his face. "Oh, is that all? I thought it was something important."

The look on Joe's face made it clear it was not a joke. "OK, Joe, I know you're serious. Where do we find this sub?"

Joe was staring out the tug's bridge windows, across Kip's Bay, at the mid-town section of Manhattan with its massive buildings. Looking west, across town on 34th Street, he could see the blue flashing lights of police cars in the distance. They were probably there to control the crowds for the parade.

"I don't know, Frank. I just don't know. Where would you drop a bomb if you had one?"

"Well, can't say I have ever done that before, but the water in this bay is pretty deep. Guess I would try to put it closer to the shoreline. But as you can see, with the heliport and the ferry piers taking up all the space along the Manhattan shoreline up to the United Nations building, it's gonna be kinda hard to squeeze in there." He paused for a moment and swung the wheel over before commenting, "Let's get out of the way of the scow coming up the river. She's gonna turn into Newton Creek and I want to give her plenty of room for the turn."

Joe scanned Newton Creek, which was no more than a hundred feet wide. He noted an old rickety barge tied up at the entrance to the creek near a large field of rocks and stones.

"What's that old barge doing over there, Frank?"

"Oh, that. The city uses the barge to store rock salt for the winter months. They can move it around to other parts of the city before a snowstorm."

"Really? Looks pretty old and rickety." Joe's lips curled. "Can you capsize her?"

Frank's eyes opened wide and his beard seemed to turn even whiter. "You're kidding right?"

"Nope. I need you to capsize her right in the middle of the bay. Can you do it?

"Sure, I can do it, but I ain't. I'll lose my license and they'll take my tug away. That's crazy talk, Joe."

Joe smiled and put his hand up on Frank's shoulder. "Actually, Frank, it's the only solution. When I was in Italy, I found out that the one thing that can stop the magneto engines on that sub is a high concentration of salt. More salt than is in the river right now. You overturn that barge in the right place, and the sub's engines will break down. If the engines break down, they can't run away. If they can't run away, they won't explode their bomb. It's easy. Let's go get the barge."

"Whoa, Joe. I'm telling you I will get into one hell of a mess if I flip that barge. You gotta get some authority for me."

"Well, Frank, in a very short time there won't be a New York, so I can assure you they won't be taking away your license or the *Ms. Charlotte*. Of course, we'll all be smoke particals at that point."

The captain turned the wheel so that the tug was now heading up river. He was stroking his craggy beard, deep in thought. "All right, but you have got to be my lawyer if this goes wrong, and I don't want to pay any legal fees."

Joe smiled and looked the captain in the eyes. "Frank, you do this and you will get a lifetime of free legal services from me – for anything. I promise. Now tell me, what is that in front of us.?"

"Oh that. Them's some rocks called Belmont. There is a navigation light tower to let ships know that the channel splits in two around Roosevelt Island. Nothing else on it but a few seagulls."

"But that's also shallow water, right? If you want the bomb to go off near the surface of the water, that would also be a good place."

"Sure, and if you look over your left shoulder, you can see it sits right in front of the U.N. buildings. In fact, they set off fireworks just behind these rocks for the United Nations when they have celebrations going on."

"Shit, that's it. That's the place. It makes sense. Both the parade and the United Nations at the same time. Frank, you're a genius. Let's get that barge."

"OK, but there's no crew on this tug today, other than the engineer below. You're gonna have to handle the tow lines. You up to it?"

Joe was already taking off his suit jacket and rolling up his sleeves. "Got a pair of gloves?"

Chapter 40
East River

"Where is the scow now?" Jian asked.

"It turned east and is headed towards that little river called…" he checked his chart, "Newton Creek. It looks like there is a plant for processing sewage there."

"Good," Jian responded. Then it appears the Americans have not located us. Are there any active vessels around us?"

Bae listened intently on his equipment. He continued to fine-tune his instruments. "Far as I can tell, there are at least four or five highspeed ferries running to or from the ferry station at 34th Street. There is a small tanker that is headed south and is over a half kilometer away. There are some more sounds of marine engines to the South, but they are too far away to identify." He readjusted his headset. "Oh, and there is a small tug that is by the entrance of Newton Creek."

"We don't have to worry about tug. It's the military ships I am worried about. There are none, correct?"

"Yes, Jian. I do not detect any military craft, although the underwater sounds being picked up by our equipment are all jumbled by the constant activity of the high-speed ferries along the piers."

"OK. Let's aim this sub towards Belmont Island. Put us on the west side of the rocks. We will drift in with the current. When the water under us is a half meter deep, we will open the bay doors."

The large screen in front of them showed a chart of New York Harbor and the East River. The blip for their sub in the center of the screen slowly moved north towards the little island of rocks. Water depth, current strength, and temperature were constantly recorded across the top of the screen. At least a half dozen green dots on the screen, representing the passenger ferries, moved quickly around the terminal area, pulling in and out of piers.

"Another hundred meters, Jian. Are the bombs ready to be lowered?"

"Yes, my friend. They are both set to go. Be assured, I have given the bombs a command to ensure that they will not detonate until two hours after they are triggered. That will give us sufficient time to escape the harbor. I know you are worried about the bombs going off while we are still here," Jian said, refusing to look over at Bae.

"Ten meters to go. Water depth is now less than twelve meters. Rising quickly." Bae slightly adjusted the joystick so that the craft compensated for the strong southerly current.

"Five, four, three, and now two meters. OK to open the bay door, but the water is real shallow and the rocks are uneven."

Jian worked at the computer keyboard at his station and began pressing keys in rapid order. A hum came from the hydraulics used to swing the two halves of the floor into the water below the sub.

Wham! The sub jolted, lifted a bit, and shook.

"What the hell was that?" demanded Jian.

"I think we scraped one of the boulders in the outcropping of the island. It is underneath us. Careful with opening the bay door."

Jian pressed the ENTER button again, and waited for the deck to fully open behind him. The gap in the floor slowly began to separate and the smell of seawater immediately hit their nostrils. The gap continued to grow, and now it was nearly two feet wide. Jian checked the rails under the two massive crates. Once the doors were opened, he would pull a lever, which would collapse the rails, allowing the two crates to drop to the seafloor. Suddenly, there was a high-pitched whine as the port-side trap door jammed. An alarm went off. It would not open!

"What the hell?" asked Jian. "The bay door is jammed. It must have been that rock we hit."

The look of fear was all over Bae's face. "You already initiated the explosion sequence on the bombs, right? Can we stop it? Tell me we can stop it!"

"First, we need to see if we can get the doors open. Help me inspect the edge of the bay doors." The two men got on their knees and felt along the edge of the door and looked into the cold dark water. After about five minutes, Jian announced he had found the problem. A large rock outside the sub was pressed up against the outside of the portside door. Since both trap doors were synchronized, both were stopped from fully opening.

"Maybe I can force the door open with a hammer," said Jian.

"Jian, shut down the bomb for now. You are taking away from the time we need to escape. Restart it when we lower the boxes to the riverbed."

The look on Jian's face was one of confusion and exasperation. Finally, he walked over to the crate on the port side and opened the panel on the side. The indigo blue lights flashed on and the keyboard slid out. Jian entered a series of keystrokes and a whirring sound was again heard. "There, that one is shut down." Jian proclaimed. "Now. Get me the hammer while I shut down the second one."

Bae started to walk carefully to the rear part of the cargo compartment when he turned to Jian and quietly said, "Don't you think you should give me the shutdown code as well? If you are hurt or incapacitated, we are both doomed."

"Very clever, my friend. You know I am the only one allowed to know the shutdown sequence. Just get me the hammer."

Bae flashed Jian a quick look of anger, but he knew his comrade was so steeped in protocol he would never change. He stepped carefully in the dark as he worked his way back to the storage cabinet.

Suddenly, the entire sub swung to the left, lifting up, and slamming down just as it began a violent roll to the right.

"What the hell?" Jian exclaimed.

On the massive screen mounted at the front of the sub, all forms of alerts were going on. For the first time, Bae noticed that a green light was almost on top of them. He made his way back to the control seat, grabbing hold of whatever he could along the way. He sat in the chair and quickly placed his headset on. He then pressed the control to lift the periscope, which Jian would never have allowed. Bae knew it was absolutely needed now. The video screen showed giant waves rolling over the rocks of what must have been Belmont Island. The white-capped waves were spraying everywhere, the backwash rolling down the rocks and crags of the island blocking the screen.. Bae rotated the periscope slowly. As the monitor continued to turn south, his mouth opened wide. He could see the beginning of a huge rusted barge, turned on its side, only a few meters from the sub. Some material inside the barge was being sucked into the water by the ebb and flood of the waves reaching into the metal hold.

"Jian, come see this!" called out Bae. There was no answer. As he continued to rotate the periscope, he again called out for Jian. There was no sign of him. Still amazed by the huge upright barge completely covering the screen, Bae got up from his seat and looked around the dark cabin for his friend. Next to the second crate, slumped on the floor, was Jian. His head was twisted. The soft glow of blue light still emanated from the small keyboard on the metal crate. Bae ran over to Jian and kneeled. He felt for a pulse in his friend's neck and checked his eyes. Bae was no doctor, but his best guess was that Jian was unconscious. Blood streaked from his hairline and covered the side of his face and shoulder. Bae stood up and looked at the keyboard. Jian had started to put in the disarm code, but only half the boxes were filled. Bae felt like saying "I told you so," but obviously his words would be wasted.

The lights in the cabin began to flicker. Bae looked around, confused. Suddenly, the giant monitor at the front of the room began to show streaks and fuzz. The picture contracted and flickered. There was a bang below deck and then another bang. Bae could only guess that the magneto engines were seizing. That had never happened. He flipped through the screens on his failing computer.

There on the top corner was the warning:

SALINITY EXCEEDS MAX – ENGINE FAILURE

Bae was astonished. As he looked at the quickly receding monitor picture, he realized that the crystal substance spilling into the water from the overturned barge was obviously salt. How had they known? Soon, the only light left in the room was the soft glow of battery-powered emergency lights, and the blue light on the second nuclear bomb that said "1:12:34" and continued to count down.

Chapter 41
Belmont Island

After they had hooked up the barge and released her from the old pier, the tug gained momentum as it headed towards Belmont Island. Joe climbed up to the top of the wheelhouse using the outside ladder. He had taken a pair of binoculars and used them to focus on the water around the rocks. With the tide starting to flow more heavily, the dark green water began to become choppy. Joe was beginning to think there was no way he could find the sub when he saw a dark blur just to the left of the first rock cropping. He refocused the lenses. There it was again. Barrett thumped on the roof of the wheelhouse and yelled, "Captain, just to the left of the first rock. About twenty feet. Bring the barge up alongside that first rock." The tug and its barge slightly changed course and moved towards the rock. Joe noticed that there were three high-speed Defender model Coast Guard rigid inflatables flying up the river with their blue lights blazing. He estimated they were still more than fifteen minutes away and probably already had the gunners strapped to the 50mm machine guns on each bow. However, fifteen minutes might be fifteen minutes too long.

Joe climbed back onto the bridge and spoke with Captain Frank about how to set the barge up against the tallest rock. It took two minutes for Joe to release the towline. He then instructed the tug captain to push the tug's bow against the side of the barge. As the tug's engines roared, the side of the barge slowly lifted and let water in over its gunwale. Once water began pouring into the barge, it quickly began to capsize, dumping the salt load into the river water. Joe could still see part of the dark shadow of the sub below the surface of the water. He was pretty certain it was not moving and that its engines had shut down. The waves from the capsizing of the barge appeared to have trapped at least one wing of the sub under some rocks. As Joe focused on the water lapping around the sub, he suddenly heard the loud warnings from the speakers on the patrol boats. As he looked up, all three patrol boats were sitting fifty yards away from the tug with their machine guns pointed at the bridge. Both Joe and Frank put up their hands so that they could clearly be seen through the windows of the tug. One Defender pulled up to the stern of the tug and two men dressed in battle gear, each holding a M-16, leaped on board. Captain Frank and Joe carefully made their way down the outside ladder to the deck, trying to keep their hands above their heads.

As Joe walked aft towards the two commandos, he shifted his eyes to towards the other side of the vessel. "The sub is under our bow. She's stuck. We capsized the barge so the salt cargo would disable the motors on the sub."

"On your knees and hands behind your back," said the closest man. The second was already on his handheld radio speaking quickly and softly.

Joe looked up and spoke again. "Speak with Chief Petty Officer Christine Milagros. My name is Joe Barrett. We have been trying to help the Coast Guard capture the sub. We have it trapped up against the rocks."

"Who told you about the sub?" demanded the commando.

"Who told us about the sub? It's the other way around. I told your superiors about the sub, the magneto motors, and the nuclear bomb." The soldier was obviously getting more suspicious. "Give me some ID. Who do you work for?"

"A law firm in New York. Please, this will go a lot faster if you contact Chief Petty Officer Milagros. I know she is in charge because she called me less than an hour ago to alert me about the sub heading up the East River and asked me how the bay doors release the bomb. Call her."

The commando looked at him with cold-steel eyes before finally turning to his comrade who was on the cell phone. The call ended a few seconds later.

"He checks out. He's been cooperating with the CG."

They let Joe and Captain Frank stand up and removed the handcuffs. Joe walked towards the bow of the tug and peered over the other side. One fin on the side of the sub could be seen just piercing the surface of the water. The image brought back memories to Joe of being in the boathouse in Portsmouth.

Joe said, "The sub is wedged in against the rock. Seems to me you ought to get one of your frogmen in there." Before Joe finished the sentence, one of the Defender crafts pulled alongside the bow of the tug and two divers immediately entered the water. Three strokes and they were standing on the sub. They carefully made their way to the closed hatch and used the butt of a pistol to rap on the hull. One diver put a device up against the hull and inserted a plug in one ear. After a few moments of intense listening, he did a thumbs up. Again, they rapped on the hull. With no answer, the diver pulled a small black box the size of a deck of cards from a pouch attached to his belt. He attached it to the center of the hatch cover before pressing a switch on the side. A red light blinked. Both divers quickly made their way back to their craft, but before they reached the low slung side of the Defender, the hatch cover to the mini-sub swung open.

Chapter 42
Kips Bay

Bae was not panicking, but things were not looking good. Jian was still lying on the deck, out cold. The blood streaking across his face and hair from the gash on his scalp was starting to slow down, but it made for a gruesome scene. Bae flipped through the pages of the manual that Jian had been holding in his hand. It did not reveal the code that had to be entered, nor was there any section on shutting down the one bomb that Jian had not yet shut down. The blue glow of the timer made clear that the clock continued to count down. There was now only one hour and twenty-nine minutes left.

The slow rocking of the sub beneath his feet meant they were stuck on the rocks and rolling with the surface waves. There would be no way to get the sub refloated; that would take a crane. The periscope continued to be blinded by the huge interior of a barge that somehow seemed to be sitting only inches from the lens. His best guess was that the barge had capsized just where the sub was positioned, crushing the sub up against and on the rocks. Jian had lost his footing and hit his head against the casing of the bomb. And for reasons that he still could not figure out, the engines had shut down due to excessive salt in the water.

Bae started to type a message to his commander in North Korea about the situation, but he soon realized that they would only criticize him for having broken radio silence. They were powerless to save him. The fact of the matter was that his superiors would much prefer that he be atomized without filing any previous complaints.

Bae's attention to the keyboard was interrupted by the sounds of footsteps on the upper surface of the sub. He estimated two or three people. Bae shrugged. It was inevitable that the U.S. Military would board the vessel. Hopefully, they would not be so foolish as to stick around and be vaporized with him.

There were two or three thumps on the hatch cover, followed by some more thumps. Someone was using a metal bar to beat the hull. Bae knew that they would not be able to open the hatch with a bar. Even with a blowtorch, it would take hours; hours that no one had. He stood up and looked over at Jian, who was still slumped on the floor and barely showing signs of breathing. Bae realized it was now time for him to do something for himself – not the motherland, not for politics, not even for his unconscious friend who would prefer to rejoin the universe as smoke. He stood under the hatch cover, entered the release code, and turned the latch. The titanium plate silently rotated and receded into the open position. Daylight poured through the opening.

Bae lowered the ladder from the ceiling cabinet, and slowly climbed the steps. The shadows of two figures standing over the hatch opening could now be seen. As he reached the top rung, two sets of hands reached down and pulled him up onto the top deck. He adjusted his eyes to the bright sunlight, the first he had seen in more than a month. As he focused his vision, the first thing he was surprised to see was the line of towering buildings running along the river's edge and the iconic outline of the United Nation's building with its green glass façade. His awe was short-lived as the man in the black wet suit in front of him, holding a weapon in his right hand, unloaded a barrage of questions in English as his companion patted Bae down and placed handcuffs on his hands. While Bae had studied some English in the North

Korean naval academy, it was a while ago. The man was talking too fast to understand, and the look on his face was anything but friendly. Bae kept looking around, and now saw the barge that was tipped on its side and pressed up against the edge of his sub. He also saw the police boats forming a wall around the little rock island, all with their blue lights flashing. Machine guns were all pointed in his direction. A beautiful, tanned metal bridge rose in the background. It spanned the entire East River, with its stone pillars rising from a pretty little island in the middle of the river that had a large green lawn and rows of trees. He continued to smile at the beautiful vista around him as the frog-man yelled into his face. When the man finally grabbed his shoulders and twisted Bae so that his face was only inches from the other man's nose, Bae's smile stopped. He looked at the man with sad eyes and simply stated in halting English, "There is a nuclear bomb in my ship. It will explode one hour twenty-five minutes. I cannot stop it."

Chapter 43
Belmont Island

Joe stepped over the rail of the tug and onto the old truck tires mounted on the bow of the *Ms. Charlotte.* From there, he gently stepped down onto the sub's dark grey and wet surface. The two Coast Guard men in front of him were questioning the small man with the broad face and nice smile who had just crawled out of the submarine. Joe could smell his body odor from five feet away. He shook his head, knowing that he would not survive for a day in the sub with his tendency towards claustrophobia. The little man looked up at him; his sad eyes struck Joe immediately. These were not the eyes of a killer to him. Yet, here he was, standing on top of an atom bomb that, in little more than an hour, would destroy hundreds of thousands of people in New York.

When Bae shifted his gaze to Joe, the Navy Seal immediately turned and stared at Joe.

"Who are you?" shouted the frogman.

"I already spoke to your superior officer on the Defender. I'm Joe Barrett, the guy who warned the Coast Guard about this sub almost two weeks ago. I have been working with Master Chief Petty Officer Milagros on locating this vehicle, and I am the one that trapped the sub by having the tug push it onto the rocks."

The man in the rubber suit told Joe not to move. He used his cell phone. He spoke in hushed tones and kept looking over at Joe. Meanwhile, Bae stared at the wonders around him. He was like a small kid marveling at all the sights in Disneyland.

The Seal turned and said, "OK, Mr. Barrett. Your story checks out, but we don't want you going anywhere. The reason we haven't gone below is our fear that the sub is booby-trapped to explode."

A slow grin built on Joe's face. "Sir, I heard him say he has a nuclear bomb down below that is going to go off in an hour and a half, and he can't stop it. I don't think there was any need for him to set a booby trap. What I am surprised by is that there is only one man. The sub is equipped to handle two in its crew."

Immediately, the big man in the wet suit turned to Bae and said, "Is that true? How many men are below? Are they armed?"

Bae concentrated on the man's lips, and after a moment of translating in his head responded, "My comrade below. He is sick, sick head," pointing to the side of his own head. "Now he sleep, how do you say, cannot wake up?"

Joe concentrated on the answer, and immediately spoke up. "You mean he is unconscious because he hurt his head?"

"Yes, unconscious. Hurt head. "

Joe's question prompted a scowl from the Marine, but the big man immediately signaled to one of the orange rigid inflatables to come alongside and provide support. Bae was ordered to sit on the deck. The Coast Guard man pulled out a flashlight and shone it down the hole into the sub. He called out, telling anyone to lie on the deck to avoid being shot. Then, he climbed down the ladder.

Barrett continued to watch the North Korean crewman. Obviously, he was not concerned about the military or the bomb on the ship. He was enjoying every minute of the Manhattan and Queens skyline. Finally, Joe spoke to the other frogman who had just helped tie up a second Coast Guard Defender to the side of the sub.

"I don't think this guy you pulled out of the sub wants to blow himself up. I think he wants to seek refuge."

"Oh, you do, do you?" was the sour response.

"Yes. He didn't come out shooting. There has been no resistance. He admitted there is a bomb. If he wanted to commit suicide, he could have sank the sub in the middle of the river and waited for it to blow. Maybe he knows who we should contact to shut off the bomb."

"Great idea, Counselor. Maybe we just call Kim Jong Jung and ask him for the shut off code. And if they give it to us we can just forget the whole thing. Brilliant, Counselor."

Joe was not going to be dismissed that easily. "Why don't you pass my idea along to Ms. Milagros. Can't hurt, and I don't think any of us has training in North Korean atomic bombs. I've got her number right here."

Before he could respond, the Seal inside the ship urgently called out for his comrade to come into the sub. The man on deck signaled someone in the second boat to come onto the sub and watch the prisoner. He also told him that Joe was not to go anywhere. As he climbed down the ladder, Joe pulled out his phone and called Milagros. It took several rings before the call was answered. Joe explained the situation and what he had overhead. Christine had already heard much of it, including Joe's presence on the sub, from the reports she was getting from the men in the area. She noted that her ship could not get under the Brooklyn bridge. She was planning on transferring to a Defender.

"Look, Christine, as I see it, you only have two options. One, stop the countdown of the bomb. Or two, get the bomb the hell out of here. I believe the Korean guy that they pulled out of the sub: he cannot stop the countdown, and he would do it if he could. He has no intention of blowing himself up. The other North Korean guy is apparently unconscious and his head is badly hurt. The only one who can get us the shut-down code is someone from North Korea. Maybe their ambassador?"

"The ambassador flew back to his country last weekend."

"Good move on his part. Well, I think you better be looking at option two real seriously and figure if you can pick this bomb up with a helicopter or something and take it as far out to sea as possible."

"We're already working on that. There should be a helo overhead in less than eight minutes. But can they get the bomb off the ship? You said the bomb hatch was on the belly of the sub."

Joe looked around and confirmed there were no seams to open the top deck of the sub. "Yeah, that's a problem. Let me get the Coast Guard guys on the phone." Barrett then called down into the open hatch and told them that Officer Milagros was on the phone and needed to speak to them immediately. The large Navy Seal took the phone as he climbed out and walked to the edge of the sub with his back turned. Joe then looked at the Bae, who was sitting on the deck, with a smile still covering his face and large eyes that were still trying to take in the view. Joe knelt down and quietly said to Bae, "How do we get the bomb out of the sub? Is there a way?"

Bae was surprised by Joe's calm voice and pleasant face. He was obviously was not a military man. Bae translated the question in his head before responding.

"Big problem. Bomb only comes out bottom of ship. Ship on rocks. No move."

Joe slowly rose to his feet, thinking over the options. He walked decisively towards the frogman who was just terminating the call. He handed the phone back to Joe.

"Look, we got to get this sub off the rocks. The bomb can only be removed through the bottom hatch. We can use the tug to pull her off. It's the only way."

"Actually, I agree with you, Mr. Barrett, but we only have minutes. Please have the tug captain get ready. I'll send someone to help you with the lines."

Barrett scampered across the sub and onto the *Ms. Charlotte*. Captain Frank was standing on bridge looking out the side window. Joe yelled something that could not be heard, but started bounding up the steps to the wheel house two at a time.

"Frank, we got to pull the sub off the rocks enough so they can open the bomb hatch."

The old bearded captain drawled, "Not sure why I would want to open any bomb doors, but I trust you know what you are doing." There was just a pause and then the captain added, "You do know what you are doing, right?"

"Sure. We drop the bomb out of the sub when it's off the rocks. A helicopter comes in and takes it far away, drops it out at sea. We all live. It's a good plan. "

"I'm sure you have calculated the weight of the bomb, the carrying capacity of the helicopter, how to hoist it up to the helicopter, whether there is a clear and open place at sea, wind speed, and its direction impacting on the helicopter – all that shit. It might make a difference as to whether I'm going to get one serious tan in about an hour."

Joe just used his hands to signal to Frank to bring the tug around to the edge of the sub, and he bounded out the wheel house door and down to the deck. He and the Coast Guardsman got the tow line on the stern ready. Joe tied a light line to the end of the tow rope and tossed it to the big guy in the dive suit on the sub, and signaled to him to start pulling. Joe then yelled to put the tow line around the stub of the starboard wing that was hung up on the rocks and then tie it off. Hopefully, one of the marines remembered how to make a bowline. The two Seals flipped the heavy rope over the sub's dorsal wing, making it look easy. Joe jogged around to the side of the tug and called up to Captain Frank to put the tug in forward very slowly. The line tightened, and the wash from the tug's big prop could be seen spewing seawater out from the stern. For a second, the *Ms. Charlotte* looked stuck herself. There was no movement forward. The two frogmen cautiously shifted their weight to the side opposite the rocks and screeching noises could be heard as the sub rubbed against the cropping. Inch by inch, it slipped back into the water and floated off the rock island.

Joe instructed Frank to stop the tug and to swing around so as to put the tug's bow up against the floating vessel so as to stop it from drifting. Joe once again leaped off the tug onto the submarine and headed to the hatch. He climbed down the vertical ladder right behind the tall marine. Inside, the body odor from trapped, recycled air was overpowering. He headed towards the pilot chairs, passing two Coastguardsmen who were attaching a harness to each canister so that the boxes could be hauled out of the water after they were dropped to the river bed.

"One hour twelve minutes" one of the men cried out. "Don't see how we can stop it."

Joe looked over the panel of instruments, briefly sitting in the command chair. He closed his eyes trying to remember what Ensign Fox had done to open that floor hatch while they were at the Boathouse in Portsmouth. Joe remembered the red button and pushed it. Then, he saw the lever at the bottom of the panel. He tried to pull it down, but it would not budge. It appeared stuck. Joe closed his eyes one more time and then remembered the shift stick maneuver that the ensign had done to engage the lever.

"OK, I'm going to pull this lever and the deck under the bombs is going to open, moving into the sidewalls. Both bombs are going to drop out of the bottom of the sub. I hope you have someone down there ready to greet those canisters?"

The Seal, nodding over his shoulder, replied, "Already done. We'll retrieve the inactive bomb later." Joe shifted the lever in the proper order, and immediately, a humming sound could be heard from under the deck. Joe watched as the floor panels pulled back from the center of the room. The dark green water of the East River could be seen lapping against the edges of the deck opening under the overhead lights built into the ceiling. Immediately, the room was filled with the odor of briny seawater. The large canisters holding the bombs surprisingly remained in place as the steel decking pulled out from under the crates. Joe noted that the shiny steel decking had beads built into the lattice surface which created almost no resistance. As the deck panels reached their maximum separation, the two crates momentarily leaned towards each other before plopping into the dark water, dropping slowly down before they disappeared. Joe checked to make sure the area was clear and then reversed the lever to close the moon pool. He was about to speak to the marine when he realized the man was already bounding up the ladder, radio in hand. Joe swiveled in the command chair, smiling at his success, until he suddenly realized that he had just positioned an atomic bomb directly below his ass. He jumped up from the comfortable seat and sprinted for the ladder.

Chapter 44
East River

The V-22 Osprey came over the Queensboro Bridge with only a few feet to spare and suddenly halted in mid-air as it approached the drama on the little island of rocks. The Osprey was not exactly a helicopter. In fact, it was referred to as a tiltrotor, capable of vertical takeoff and landing. The otherwise normal-looking aircraft had wings and two large engines that rotated ninety degrees into a kind of helicopter position. When the wings returned to a normal position, the Osprey flew like any other plane. Indeed, its advantage was that it could fly at almost two-hundred-fifty miles per hour, almost twice the speed of a helicopter, and it could carry nearly ten tons of cargo.

Joe watched as the large wings suddenly began to rotate and the huge fan blades on each side of the aircraft twisted up towards the sky. The wash from the propellers turned the surface of the river into a crazy froth of white foam. Slowly, the plane began to descend and then hovered about fifty feet over the little submarine. Its bay doors opened, and a heavy-looking metal cable was lowered by someone wearing a red helmet and flight suit. Joe noticed that one of the scuba divers was now on the surface of the water and used his hands to signal the cable's descent. Moments after it hit the water's surface, the diver grabbed it. He submerged immediately and took the cable underwater. For nearly four minutes, the plane remained hovering in position, the engines emitting a thunderous roar as the huge props ripped the air. A moment later, the diver popped his head out of the water. Holding the cable, he gave a thumbs-up sign. The helmeted man in the bay door waved back and turned his head as the diver swam towards the red-colored Coast Guard boat. Joe could hear the propellers gaining speed. The downward wash of the air blast from the Osprey made the surface of the water bubble and foam. Droplets of seawater spit everywhere, stinging Joe's face. Slowly, the aircraft rose, the cable stretch taut below it. Joe was nudged by an officer standing next to him, pointing in the direction of an area of water that was beginning to rise like a fountain. The metal case broke through the surface. The straps around the box were obviously straining, and water was now pouring off the top surface. There seemed to be a momentary jerk, and then the bomb case broke free of the East River. Rivulets of water streamed behind as the box slowly rose above them. Joe could now see the wings slowly rotate forward on the Osprey, giving the craft forward momentum. It continued to pick up speed and made a slow ascent into the sky.

"I thought they were going to load the case into the aircraft," Joe said to the officer.

"Too dangerous and it would just take more time. We want to use every second to get that thing as far out to sea as possible."

Joe watched as the aircraft with the small box dangling below it increased altitude and disappeared over the Williamsburg Bridge.

"Will they be able to drop it far enough out at sea?" queried Joe. "Well, we are down to fifty-two minutes," he responded, looking at his watch. "They should be a little over two hundred miles out when it's dropped into the sea. My hope is that it will submerge at least at thousand feet into the Atlantic rift when it goes off. There'll be a hell of a hole in the ocean for a few minutes, but I think that, other than the terrible damage to the marine ecology, we should be OK.

The wind is blowing east, out to sea, and rain is expected this evening. Fallout should be minimal. Let's just hope the timer on the bomb was accurate." He paused for a second, and then looked at Joe. "Can we give you a lift home, Mr. Barrett? You have done your country one hell of a service today."

Joe smiled, perhaps for the first time that day. "Got the *Ms. Charlotte* waiting for me. I'll be OK. Think I'll head home and wait for the boom." He shook the officer's hand before stepping quickly back onto the tug. Joe walked up to the pilot house and greeted Frank with a tired look on his face.

"Captain, one last request. Can you drop me off at the pier in Astoria? It's time to head home."

"Aye, Joe. That it is." The tug came to life and rumbled as it backed away from the sub. A half dozen Coast Guard men were now on the craft securing it for tow. For the first time, Joe noticed that thousands of people were lined up and watching the event along the FDR highway on the edge of Manhattan and at the tip of Roosevelt Island. They will probably never know how close they came to oblivion, he thought. As the tug made its way slowly up the east channel of the River, Joe felt his phone ring in his pocket. He picked it up but did not recognize the number.

"Hello?"

"Joe, this is Christine. I just spoke with one of the officers on the submarine. Without your tug and your knowledge of the bay doors, well, I don't want to think about what could have happened. Thank you. I really mean it."

"Christine, the credit goes to you for having listened to me weeks ago with my crackpot theory. But if you don't mind, I'm headed home to see my fiancé and give her a hug. After today, I'm going back to practicing law. It's a lot safer."

Christine could be heard laughing on the other end of the phone, and simply said goodbye to Joe. No sooner was the line disconnected than Joe dialed Dalia.

"Joe, are you alright?" she anxiously answered.

"Yup. I think we are all going to be OK. Where are you now?"

"I am just over the Connecticut borderline. Traffic is suddenly getting heavy. What should I do?"

Joe laughed, "Turn around and come home. Everything is safe now. You might hear something that sounds like thunder in about a half-hour. Ignore it. Can't wait to see you."

"Alright. I'll turn around at the next exit. See you at home. Love you." Joe put his cell phone back in his pocket and leaned against the bridge window. He watched the wisps of smoke from two of the stacks at the Ravenswood power plant rise straight up into the air, until they blended with the puffy clouds. Captain Frank kept his tug on the scene until the Coast Guard said he could leave the area. He then navigated across the bay and neatly brought the blue and white tug alongside the ferry terminal at the edge of Astoria. Passengers waiting for the next water ferry stared at the old tug and its single rider. As he stepped off the tug onto the concrete pier, holding a piling to steady himself, there was a momentary flash of white-light high in the sky, followed by a loud crack and distant rumble through the air. Dozens of seagulls simultaneously flew off their perches, shrieking to one another. Joe did not turn around. He walked off the pier onto the sidewalk along Vernon Boulevard and waited to flag down a cab.

Epilogue

Dabbled sunlight bounced off the seasick-green colored walls in Joe's office. The shades were partly drawn to keep down the glare on a cloudless winter day. Steam rose from a half-empty cup of coffee sitting on the cover of a law book, only inches from the crossed feet that were resting on top of the mahogany attorney's desk. Brown boat shoes dangled from the sockless feet. Joe was leaning back at a precarious angle in his worn armchair reading The New York Times. A photograph, probably taken from the gardens of the United Nations overlooking the East River, showed several men standing, almost miraculously, on top of the water near the edge of Roosevelt Island. The grey hull of the sub blended in with the muddled colors of the East River. The navigational tower on Belmont Island could be seen in the background, just behind the three men, as well as an old tug boat and a capsized barge. Coast Guard and police boats surrounded the scene, while an awkward-looking aircraft hung in the air with its huge propellers swiveled straight up into the sky. If one looked very closely at the pixels near the center of the photo, there was a tall athletic man in a loose-fitting business suit talking to several men dressed in orange-colored fatigues. The caption below the photo failed to identify the man, and only noted that "there were several people from the Coast Guard present."

Hiding the atomic blast from the news media had proved impossible. The sonic blast was heard for hundreds of miles. Fishing vessels, who had been warned to stay away from a certain area in the Atlantic, had witnessed something of a fireball on the horizon and a muted mushroom cloud.

Colombia University's seismic instruments recorded the full impact of the event out at sea. What most people had not known was that the coastline had been spared the impact of a tsunami wave after the explosion because the bomb detonated well below the walls of the Hudson canyon, a submarine trench that extended about four hundred miles into the Atlantic ocean. The walls of the canyon were nearly three-quarters of a mile high, competing with the Grand Canyon.

The government only stated that "there was an accident." The never-ending heads of commentators on CNN, of course, all had theories about how this was a government cover-up given the unexplainable activity that was spotted on the East River only minutes before the explosion. The box dangling from the fleeing aircraft was a dead giveaway to a possible source of the explosion. One expert after another was marched before the television cameras to give their estimate as to significant loss of life and property that could have been experienced if the explosion had happened inside the city, especially on Thanksgiving Day. More experts were called in to explain the odd shape of the watercraft that was spotted in the East River, and was ultimately towed away by the Coast Guard. The more the news media dug, the more the government sources became silent.

Ken walked into Joe's office with Dalia, as usual, not bothering to knock. Joe looked up from the folded pages and smiled.

Ken sat in one of the wobbly guest chairs and looked up at his boss. "Must feel pretty good to have saved the world, huh?" Dalia chuckled, and took the other chair.

"I am so happy to be back in the office," Joe replied, and then looked under his desk, "especially knowing there are no bombs nearby."

At that moment, Tim poked his head through the door.

"Heh, did you hear the latest? The United Nations is scheduling an emergency session of its Security Council. Looks like both Jian and Bae are going to testify about their mission to blow up New York, including the U.N."

"Wonder what is going to happen?" asked Dalia. "There is already a joint military fleet sailing towards North Korea. Last thing we need is war."

Ken cleared his throat and remarked, "I suspect this will put pressure on the young dictator to step down. Otherwise, his country is going to be isolated into the Stone Age. And China won't be able to help this time. They got enough explaining to do themselves. It could be that, for the first time, we will really have some world peace."

A tall figure stood behind Tim and gently coughed. It was Alistair McDowell, the firm's Managing Partner. Tim immediately stepped out into the hallway to give the senior partner some room.

"Joe," said McDowell, "the firm is obviously very proud of the role you and your team played in, ahh, keeping us safe." It was obvious he was looking for the right words. "I understand that you will be called to Washington for a debriefing. That is fine with us. Take Dalia with you. You two deserve some time off." He scratched his head and then looked down at Dalia. "By the way, has a date been set? My wife and I would not miss the wedding for the world."

"You'll be the first to know," she responded. "We want to invite everyone, isn't that right, Joe?"

"Great," responded McDowell as he turned to leave the room. "But you better check your future husband out before you march down the aisle. I suspect he will be wearing those same boat shoes at the wedding." Joe quickly took his feet off the desk and smiled sheepishly.

ABOUT THE AUTHOR

Vince DeOrchis has been a practicing maritime lawyer in New York City for nearly forty-seven years. Before going to law school, he spent several months at sea as a deckhand on a freighter that traveled between Spain and the East Coast of the US. In the course of handling many marine casualty cases, he has traveled around the world performing investigations and working with organizations like the Comite Maritime International, the Maritime Law Association of the US, and the UNCITRAL workshop involved in the development of a new international convention for the carriage of cargo at sea. The author is also one of the founders of the International Maritime Law Seminar, which takes place each year in London and Singapore.

The author lives in Centerport, Long Island with his wife. He is an avid sailor, proficient at art glass and an admitted amateur painter. His son and daughter live in the New York area, giving him time to play with his three granddaughters.

www.ingramcontent.com/pod-product-compliance
Lightning Source LLC
LaVergne TN
LVHW090318210926
848480LV00001B/286